Badhai

FORMS OF DRAMA

Forms of Drama meets the need for accessible, mid-length volumes that offer undergraduate readers authoritative guides to the distinct forms of global drama. From classical Greek tragedy to Chinese pear garden theatre, cabaret to *kathakali*, the series equips readers with models and methodologies for analysing a wide range of performance practices and engaging with these as "craft".

SERIES EDITOR: SIMON SHEPHERD

Badhai

Hijra-Khwaja Sira-Trans
Performance across Borders
in South Asia

Adnan Hossain,
Claire Pamment,
and Jeff Roy

methuen | drama

LONDON · NEW YORK · OXFORD · NEW DELHI · SYDNEY

METHUEN DRAMA
Bloomsbury Publishing Plc
50 Bedford Square, London, WC1B 3DP, UK
1385 Broadway, New York, NY 10018, USA
29 Earlsfort Terrace, Dublin 2, Ireland

BLOOMSBURY, METHUEN DRAMA and the Methuen Drama logo are
trademarks of Bloomsbury Publishing Plc

First published in Great Britain 2023
This paperback edition published 2024

For legal purposes the Acknowledgements on pp. xviii–xix constitute an
extension of this copyright page.

Series design by Charlotte Daniels

A catalogue record for this book is available from the British Library.

Library of Congress Cataloging-in-Publication Data
Names: Hossain, Adnan, author. | Pamment, Claire, author. |
Roy, Jeff (College teacher) author.
Title: Badhai : Hijra-Khwaja Sira-Trans performance across borders in South Asia
/ Adnan Hossain, Claire Pamment and Jeff Roy.
Description: London ; New York : Methuen Drama 2023. |
Series: Forms of drama | Includes bibliographical references and index.
Identifiers: LCCN 2022018278 (print) | LCCN 2022018279 (ebook) |
ISBN 9781350174535 (hardback) | ISBN 9781350346024 (paperback) |
ISBN 9781350174542 (epub) | ISBN 9781350174559 (ebook)
Subjects: LCSH: Performing arts–South Asia. |
Transgender people–South Asia.
Classification: LCC PN2860 .H366 2023C:\Users\trod\AppData\Local\Temp\
VALID.BIB (print) | LCC PN2860 (ebook) | DDC 792.095–dc23/eng/20220711
LC record available at https://lccn.loc.gov/2022018278
LC ebook record available at https://lccn.loc.gov/2022018279

ISBN: HB: 978-1-3501-7453-5
        PB: 978-1-3503-4602-4
        ePDF: 978-1-3501-7455-9
        eBook: 978-1-3501-7454-2

Series: Forms of Drama

Typeset by Integra Software Services Pvt. Ltd.

To find out more about our authors and books visit www.bloomsbury.com and
sign up for our newsletters.

CONTENTS

LIST OF FIGURES

SERIES PREFACE

The scope of this series is scripted aesthetic activity that works by means of personation.

Scripting is done in a wide variety of ways. It may, most obviously, be the more or less detailed written text familiar in the stage play of the western tradition, which not only provides lines to be spoken but directions for speaking them. Or it may be a set of instructions, a structure or scenario, on the basis of which performers improvise, drawing, as they do so, on an already learnt repertoire of routines and responses. Or there may be nothing written, just sets of rules, arrangements, and even speeches orally handed down over time. The effectiveness of such unwritten scripting can be seen in the behaviour of audiences, who, without reading a script, have learnt how to conduct themselves appropriately at the different activities they attend. For one of the key things that unwritten script specifies and assumes is the relationship between the various groups of participants, including the separation, or not, between doers and watchers.

What is scripted is specifically an aesthetic activity. That specification distinguishes drama from non-aesthetic activity using personation. Following the work of Erving Goffman in the mid-1950s, especially his book *The Presentation of Self in Everyday Life*, the social sciences have made us richly aware of the various ways in which human interactions are performed. Going shopping, for example, is a performance in that we present a version of ourselves in each encounter we make. We may indeed have changed our clothes before setting out. This, though, is a social performance.

The distinction between social performance and aesthetic activity is not clear-cut. The two sorts of practice overlap and mingle with one another. An activity may be more or less aesthetic, but the crucial distinguishing feature is the status of the aesthetic element. Going shopping may contain an aesthetic element – decisions about clothes and shoes to wear – but its purpose is not deliberately to make an aesthetic activity or to mark itself as different from everyday social life. The aesthetic element is not regarded as a general requirement. By contrast a court-room trial may be seen as a social performance, in that it has an important social function, but it is at the same time extensively scripted, with prepared speeches, costumes, and choreography. This scripted aesthetic element assists the social function in that it conveys a sense of more than everyday importance and authority to proceedings which can have life-changing impact. Unlike the activity of going shopping the aesthetic element here is not optional. Derived from tradition it is a required component that gives the specific identity to the activity.

It is defined as an activity in that, in a way different from a painting of Rembrandt's mother or a statue of Ramesses II, something is made to happen over time. And, unlike a symphony concert or firework display, that activity works by means of personation. Such personation may be done by imitating and interpreting—'inhabiting'—other human beings, fictional or historical, and it may use the bodies of human performers or puppets. But it may also be done by a performer who produces a version of their own self, such as a stand-up comedian or court official on duty, or by a performer who, through doing the event, acquires a self with special status as with the *hijras* securing their sacredness by doing the ritual practice of *badhai*.

Some people prefer to call many of these sorts of scripted aesthetic events not drama but cultural performance. But there are problems with this. First, such labelling tends to keep in place an old-fashioned idea of western scholarship that drama, with its origins in ancient Greece, is a specifically European 'high' art. Everything outside it is then potentially, and damagingly, consigned to a domain which may be neither 'art' nor 'high'. Instead the European stage play and its like can best be regarded as a subset of the general category, distinct from the rest in that two groups of people come together in order specifically to present and watch a story being acted out by imitating other persons and settings. Thus the performance of a stage play in this tradition consists of two levels of activity using personation: the interaction of audience and performers and the interaction between characters in a fictional story.

The second problem with the category of cultural performance is that it downplays the significance and persistence of script, in all its varieties. With its roots in the traditional behaviors and beliefs of a society, script gives specific instructions for the form – the materials, the structure, and sequence – of the aesthetic activity, the drama. So too, as we have noted, script defines the relationships between those who are present in different capacities at the event.

It is only by attending to what is scripted, to the form of the drama, that we can best analyse its functions and pleasures. At its most simple, analysis of form enables us to distinguish between different sorts of aesthetic activity. The masks used in *kathakali* look different from those used in commedia dell'arte. They are made of different materials, designs, and colours. The roots of those differences lie in their separate cultural traditions and systems of living. For similar reasons the puppets of *karagoz* and *wayang* differ. But perhaps more importantly the attention to form provides a basis for exploring the operation and effects of a particular work. Those who regularly participate in and watch drama, of whatever sort, learn to recognize and remember the forms of what they see and hear. When one drama has family resemblances to another, in its organization and use of materials, structure, and sequences, those who attend it develop expectations as to how it will—or indeed should—operate. It then becomes possible to specify how a particular work subverts, challenges, or enhances these expectations.

Expectation doesn't only govern response to individual works, however. It can shape, indeed has shaped, assumptions about which dramas are worth studying. It is well established that Asia has ancient and rich dramatic traditions, from the Indian sub-continent to Japan, as does Europe, and these are studied with enthusiasm. But there is much less widespread activity, at least in western universities, in relation to the traditions of, say, Africa, Latin America, and the Middle East. Secondly, even within the recognized traditions, there are assumptions that some dramas are more 'artistic', or indeed more 'serious', 'higher' even, than others. Thus it may be assumed that *noh* or classical tragedy will require the sort of close attention to craft which is not necessary for mumming or *badhai*.

Both sets of assumptions here keep in place a system which allocates value. This series aims to counteract a discriminatory value system by ranging as widely as possible across world practices and by giving the same sort of attention to all the forms it features. Thus book-length studies of forms such as *al-halqa*, *hana keaka* and *ta'zieh* will appear in English for perhaps the first time. Those studies, just like those of *kathakali*, tragicomedy, and the rest, will adopt the same basic approach. That approach consists of an historical overview of the development of a form combined with, indeed anchored in, detailed analysis of examples and case studies. One of the benefits of properly detailed analysis is that it can reveal the construction which gives a work the appearance of being serious, artistic, and indeed 'high'.

What does that work of construction is script. This series is grounded in the idea that all forms of drama have script of some kind and that an understanding of drama, of any sort, has to include analysis of that script. In taking this approach, books in this series again challenge an assumption that has in recent times governed the study of drama. Deriving from the supposed, but artificial, distinction between cultural performance and drama, many accounts of cultural performance ignore its scriptedness and assume that the proper way of studying it is simply to describe how its practitioners behave and what they make. This is useful enough, but to leave it at that is to produce something that looks like a form of lesser anthropology. The description of behaviors is only the first step in that it establishes what the script is. The next step is to analyse how the script and form work and how they create effect.

But it goes further than this. The close-up analyses of materials, structures, and sequences—of scripted forms—show how they emerge from and connect deeply back into the modes of life and belief to which they are necessary. They tell us in short why, in any culture, the drama needs to be done. Thus by adopting the extended model of drama, and by approaching all dramas in the same way, the books in this series aim to tell us why, in all societies, the activities of scripted aesthetic personation – dramas – keep happening, and need to keep happening.

I am grateful, as always, to Mick Wallis for helping me to think through these issues. Any clumsiness or stupidity is entirely my own.

Simon Shepherd

FOREWORD

In the burgeoning literature on dissident genders in South Asia, *Badhai: Hijra-Khwaja Sira-Trans Performance across Borders in South Asia* is a collective offering that stands out. Co-authored by Adnan Hossain, Claire Pamment, and Jeff Roy, it centers performance—and specifically, the generative acts of *badhai*—to re-envision *hijra-khwaja sira-trans* pasts, presents, and futures across boundaries of nation, genre, and discipline. Drawing from their individual work in Bangladesh, Pakistan, and India, their different sensory foci as well as disciplinary locations of anthropology, theater and film studies, and performance and sound studies, the authors deploy collaborative writing to co-produce this important volume; the process as much as the product serves as an intentional provocation to think and do otherwise.

Badhai uses performance as a lever through which to pry open the landscape of *hijra-khwaja sira-trans* studies in South Asia, productively reorienting our gaze to tell other histories, other stories. It reveals the stakes of centering *badhai* as a mode and medium through which to stage the interconnections across, between, and through region and relationality. In this process, performance emerges polyvocally as a connective tissue, portal, and method.

While attentive to the specifics of locality and context, Hossain, Pamment, and Roy simultaneously remap the contours of geography, history, and performance in this volume to tell an alternative story not just of *hijra*, *khwaja sira*, and *trans* lives in South Asia, but of the possibilities of desires, inter-corporeal exchanges, and sensorial orientations that are best analyzed across national boundaries, across performance genres, across disciplines, and in relation to each other. As such, one of the most generative contributions of this volume is its articulation of performance, and specifically, the embodied enactment of *badhai*, as an inter-relational connective framework, a ligament suturing multiple spaces, publics, and performances. The most obvious of these connections, of course, is the volume's regional orientation, following the recent turn to regional analyses in anthropology, area studies, queer, and performance/visual studies, to name just a few intellectual formations. This pivot pushes against the nation/nationalism as well as easy invocations of transnationalism as primary if not sole frames for understanding the nexus between gender, sexuality, and place. *Badhai* reorients our analysis across national boundaries to South Asia, a region that is linked not solely by colonial pasts, but also by neoliberal presents, and religious futures. As Hossain, Pamment, and Roy highlight, not only do *badhai* practices in this region reflect a plurality of interconnected origin narratives, tropes, gestures, linguistic, and religious referents that cross geo-political boundaries, they also reveal the possibilities of examining the artifice of the nation and its boundaries, allowing us to understand the heterogeneity of a coherent regional *hijrascape*. Simultaneously, this volume also pushes back against the myopias of a colonial visual regime that decentered performance and focused solely on the abject regulations of dissident *hijra-khwaja sira-trans* bodies. Even as Hossain, Pamment, and Roy emphasize the temporal continuities between colonial and postcolonial regimes which hierarchize and criminalize embodied performance acts by *hijras*, *khwaja siras*, and *trans* bodies, this volume also reflects the textures, tenors, as well as pleasures of agentive doing across multiple boundaries—including nation and state, public and domestic, Hindu and Muslim, aesthetic and affective, *badhai* and *cholla*, visual and sonic – embracing *hijras* and *khwaja siras*' creative deployments of *badhai* to disrupt, improvise, and engender anew in the process.

Through these connections, performance becomes a portal through which to reframe existing narratives about *hijra* and *khwaja sira* histories and authenticating tropes. For example, one retelling that this volume facilitates is destabilizing the narrative of *badhai* as an ahistorical "tradition" in *hijra-khwaja sira-trans* lives. As the authors point out, much of the extant literature— including my book—depict *badhai* as a largely static "ritual role" that is both temporally and categorically at odds with "modern" logics of postcolonial state and capital insertion. Through this volume, *badhai* emerges instead as a living, breathing aspect of *hijra* and *khwaja sira* worldmaking, very much imbricated in their everyday enactments and engendering of social and economic life. *Badhai* animates *hijra* and *khwaja sira* lives; through performance, it brings into being, every day, the worlds that *hijras*, *khwaja siras*, and their many publics occupy.

Finally, this volume creatively deploys performance as method, tracing the polyvocality and potential of performance practices to capture, generate, and sustain subaltern counter publics. It does so by radically engaging with others both in the field and on the page, in the collective labor of co-producing this volume. It articulates, through the vibrant soundscapes and performance practices of *badhai* in Bangladesh, Pakistan, and India that the authors engage in *with* their interlocutors, what Dwight Conquergood referred to as "co-performative witnessing." This evocative phrase captures what it means to be "radically engaged and committed … a politics of the body deeply in action with Others" as Soyini Madison phrases it, quoting Conquergood (Madison 2007: 826). This co-performative and collective praxis allows us to not only witness what *badhai* does, and is, for its practitioners, interlocutors, and their various publics, but the very act of writing this text could be interpreted as a radical act of such dialogic performance.

What emerges from this collaborative labor is an embodied text that asks us to sit with difference productively. *Badhai* allows us to see, hear, and feel the mutually imbricated logics of place, performance, and publics through a different register. In so doing, much like a kaleidoscope, it changes the picture, enlivening our understanding not merely of *hijra*, *khwaja sira*, and *trans* lives, but also the play of performance in engendering alternative visions of pasts, presents, and futures in South Asia.

It is my tremendous honor and privilege to write this preface for Adnan Hossain, Claire Pamment, and Jeff Roy's *Badhai: Hijra-Khwaja Sira-Trans Performance across Borders in South Asia*—a book that embraces the promiscuity and potential of *badhai* to gift us a new lens through which to see *hijra-khwaja sira-trans* (and academic) worldmaking in South Asia.

Gayatri Reddy
University of Illinois Chicago

ACKNOWLEDGEMENTS

We thank collaborating *badhai* practitioners and publics, Jessica Hinchy, Kareem Khubchandani, Queer South Asia Symposium Collective, Gayatri Reddy, Simon Shepherd, Southwest Conference on Asian Studies, Ella Wilson and the editors at Methuen Drama.

Adnan thanks Abba, Amma, Graduate Gender Program, Utrecht University, Jomuna (Rest in Peace), Joya, Katha, Kala, Mengdu, Mousumi, Mukti, Safwana, Shipon, Suhaila, Srabonti, Sumaiya, Tuku Munshi, Yousuf.

Claire thanks Nicholas Abbott, Amber, American Institute of Pakistan Studies, Darvish, Imran Anwar, Arzu, Choti Ashee, Muneera Batool, Bholi, Anmol Bukhari, Ashee Butt, Saima Butt, Billi, Coco Fellowship, Deviya, Sanum Faqir, Naghma Gogi, Goshi, Qasim Iqbal, Ami Kabutri (*mahroom*), Shahnaz Khan, Khwaja Sira Society, Knapsack Studios, Maham, Guru Nadeem, Nanni, Hamza Abbas Malik, Hajji Nargis, Naz Pakistan, Nukhbat Malik, Olomopolo Media, Neeli Rana, Anaya Rahimi, Reema Jaan, Sana, Iram Sana, Sarmad Sehbai, Sheela, Sonia, The Social Sciences and Humanities Research Council of Canada, team *Teesri Dhun*, William & Mary.

Jeff thanks Priyamvad and their beloved queer family, Abheena Aher and the Dancing Queens, Aiza and the Miya Gharana, American Institute for Indian Studies, Prince Manvendra Singh Gohil, Divya (*Om Shanti*), Film Independent, Fulbright-Hays, Fulbright-mtvU, Godrej India Culture Lab, Humsafar Trust, India HIV/AIDS Alliance, Urmi Jadhav, Kashish Mumbai International Queer Film Festival, Omar Kasmani, Shivananda Khan (Rest in Peace), Madhuri, Naz

Foundation International, Nishant, Anuja Parikh, Pavithra Prasad, Rumya Putcha, Sridhar Rangayan, James Robertson, Saumya, Juneeta Singh, Society for Ethnomusicology, Solaris Pictures, University of California, Los Angeles, and Cal Poly Pomona.

Introduction

Adnan Hossain,
Claire Pamment, and Jeff Roy

"Bismillah! May Allah give you more! May He protect you and give you happiness," the performers call while knocking at the door of a household celebrating a wedding. Sensing the household's tepid response, the musicians start up a lively Punjabi folk song, and the khwaja sira performers fill the hitherto quiet street with dance. Gradually, curious faces line rooftops and doorways, and the performers flirtatiously gesture the bystanders into their song, singing: "Oh my beautiful has come [...] but I am not going to talk to him who is mean to us." Pulled into the music and dance, and the feelings of the street, the celebrant householders open their door and are moved to dance.—A scene from Lahore, Punjab, Pakistan (2014)

The manjeera (two small metal cymbals) on the higher end of the sonic register, the dholak (two-headed drum) on the lower end, ghungroo (ankle bells), and clapping in the middle form an interlaced, rhythmic trellis upon which the melody, carried by the voice, grows. With them comes a sensation of being lifted. In the final tihai (three-part rhythmic refrain),

*the voices call on the presence of the goddess in this place,
orienting listeners and doers towards the possibility of being
blessed. "Please come with all your glory, oh Bahuchara Mata
(hijra goddess), I'm yearning to meet you; That's all I want;
Through my throat you sing!"*—Scenes from Surat, Gujarat
and Kalyan, Maharashtra, India (2011; in Roy 2015a: 198)

*"We have a license from the government to demand badhai
until the child is five years old!"—shout Josna, Jerin and
Jhumi in chorus to the householder who refuses to open the
door and let them in stating that the child is no longer a
newborn as he is one year old. The man, visibly agitated,
proceeds to draw their attention to the fact that it is the house
of a local imam (a Muslim religious leader who leads the
prayers), and that they should leave and come another time
when he is home. Jhumi chimes in suggesting that because
the imam earns throughout the year and is rich, he should
look after people like them who are Allah's creation. In the
meantime, bystanders congregate, requesting the troupe to
sing a song and play the dhol (drum), but the hijras steadfastly
refuse since they have not received any payment. The imam
appears on the scene minutes later and pays the troupe 1000
taka.*—A scene from Dhaka, Bangladesh (2016).

Badhai includes songs, dances, prayers, comic repartee,
gesture, touch, intimacies, shock, and/or spectacle that
customarily commemorate births, weddings, and other
celebratory occasions marking important financial and/
or heteronormative occasions across areas of Bangladesh,
India, Pakistan, and beyond. Appearing in a multiplicity of
South Asian languages, *badhai* or *vadhai* (Punjabi) means
"gift" and is imbricated in webs of reciprocities between
performers, ensembles, their lineages and publics. Performed
by *hijra*, *khwaja sira*, and *trans* communities[1]—socially
marginalized along the lines of gender, sexuality, class, caste,
and religion—*badhai* interacts with a variety of people in a
range of spaces, from open streets and shops, to courtyards of
houses and private domestic spaces. Performers learn and tune

their repertoire to the particular composition of the troupe, often comprised of singers, dancers, and musicians (who in some contexts are also drawn from outside of immediate *hijra-khwaja sira-trans* communities), and their publics, in intercorporeal exchanges that operate on a spectrum of familiar scripts and spontaneous tactics. These immersive performance experiences are improvisational, responsive to the particularities of the group, the context of the occasion, the site itself, and the willingness (or otherwise) of patrons, which is often contingent on their level of familiarity with *badhai* practices. Whether through instant observation or knowledge cultivated by particular households over time, performers play with, across, and off their publics' genders, sexualities, class, castes, economic status, religious compositions, abilities, and other sociocultural relationalities. No two performances look and/or sound the same even by the same group, let alone by groups in different regions or countries, and yet they resonate across borders of South Asia.

In this collaboratively authored book, we engage in transgressive travel within, across, and against boundaries of nations, disciplines, and genres. We reorient previous mappings of *badhai* practices, which have been embedded in colonial criminalization, religious and/or neoliberal nationalisms, abject othering, fetishization, and classist framings of "art" in scholarship. We analyze *badhai*'s promiscuous, and sometimes precarious, traffickings in and across borders of South Asia through the changing landscapes of transnational LGBTQIA+ and liberal rights-based social movements, in which practices of self-and-other labeling, as well as the regulation of institutions and categories, are contested in different ways. *Hijra*, *khwaja sira*, and transgender are employed alongside numerous nomenclatures that continue to circulate throughout South Asia. We employ the term *hijra-khwaja sira-trans* to highlight the interconnected networks of communication spanning boundaries of nations. Working across the changing landscapes of identity and culture, we engage performance—its embodiments, sensorial orientations, affective possibilities, politics, and changing economies—in order to highlight the movements and flows against, through, and across boundaries of understanding *badhai*. These movements inform our approach to collaborative authorship as we draw from our insights and work in anthropology, theater and performance studies, sound studies, ethnomusicology, queer studies, and over a decade of field work about and with *hijra-khwaja sira-trans* communities in areas of Bangladesh, Pakistan, and India. Our collective writing of the introduction and individually-authored chapters highlight the intimate ways we are each embedded in a particular place while illuminating points of alignment and divergence that occur through transcultural contact and communication across the *hijrascape*,[2] what we collectively refer to as the multi-layered, multi-scalar, and multisensorial movements and flows that constitute *hijra-khwaja sira-trans* relationalities, lifeworlds, and imaginaries within and across different cultures and societies.

Our collaboration crosses symbolic, physical, and sensorial boundaries, drawing from distinct and shared practices of history, culture, and performance specific to a given context in the *hijrascape*. In our chapters, we each bring different experiences, conceptualizations, critique, and access points to our studies of *badhai*. For instance, Hossain's experience serving a legal/financial intermediary role in Bangladeshi *hijra* communities informs his study on the economics of communication and performance across changing political and legal terrain. Pamment's devised theater-making and film projects with *khwaja sira* and *trans* performers in Pakistan informs her foregrounding affect and relationalities of these intercorporeal performances in continually shifting landscapes, particularly around transgender rights. Roy's music and filmmaking with *trans-hijra* performers in India bring into focus the affective, sensorial, and political possibilities of *badhai* sonic arrangements in differently contested spaces. While illuminating different positional, theoretical, and methodological orientations, these chapters chart important place-based features and contexts informing *badhai* repertoire, social networks, and practices. This introduction provides an overview of *badhai*'s materialities in performance, the legacies of the colonial visual regime in *hijra-khwaja sira-trans* studies, and our proposed interventions based on the critiques highlighted therein.

Contexts of Performance

While the contexts and elements of performance shape *badhai* across South Asia, they also provide a shifting lexicon through which performance is experienced and innovated. *Badhai* draws from the lifeworld of the *dera* (home) and its lineage networks, through collective labor that plays an important role in its cultural and material economy. This section introduces the *dera* and its lineages, and how they impart a plurality of performance repertoires, ensembles, and publics spanning religion, language, and geo-political boundaries.

*Dera*s and Lineages

The *dera*, presided over by a *guru* (teacher/parent), offers many *chela*s (disciples/children) a refuge from "unhomely" natal families and a new home beyond the systemic violence of cisheteronormative society. Careful not to romanticize the *dera*, which for some entails its own violence and hierarchies, Hamzić describes its liminal qualities, as an anchor of "spatial and identitary journeying towards collective *thereness*" (2019: 36; citing Sutherland 2018). In contexts where cisheteronormative homes may have punished self-expression, *badhai*, which demands its practitioners to enter and perform in public spaces, often facilitates journeys where *hijra-khwaja sira-trans* people find opportunities for personal expression and growth. The *dera* is a physical home and also offers a spiritual homing, passed down through a lineage of community elders or *guru*s. The collective work of *badhai* plays a significant role in providing for household expenses, strengthening kinship bonds, and continuing the labor of *guru*s, present and past. Participating in the primary organizational and pedagogical system known widely as the *guru–chela* (teacher–disciple) relationship, *chela*s learn *badhai* from *guru*s largely through immersive embodied experiences consolidated through regular practice both in the field and at community gatherings (Roy 2015a: 11–13). Reciprocally, *chela*s practicing *badhai* demonstrate "service" to the *guru* and a commitment to the *dera* that cultivates *izzat* ("respect"; Reddy 2005: 43). In turn, those who demonstrate commitment and *izzat* to the *dera* are invariably promoted in rank, which can lead to the *guru* transferring responsibilities of governance. Not all *badhai* practitioners are physical residents of the *dera*. Likewise, not all residents of the *dera* perform *badhai*. Those who practice *badhai* alongside other forms of labor (with or without their *guru*s' consent) may take up occupations as multifarious as the subjectivities that comprise these communities, from professional dancing, to agricultural work, tailoring, sex work, NGO work, and other professions. In the reciprocal economy of the *dera*, notions of *izzat* may be fluid depending on the relations between *guru*s and *chela*s, and their relations in the lineage.

The *dera* is often embedded in wider lineages—sometimes called *gharana*, *ghor/ghar*, *silsila*, or *line*—networks of extended kinship which might span an area of the city, province, and sometimes across national borders of South Asia, and even elsewhere. These lineages offer protection, social and financial support, mutual accountability, conflict arbitration, and are overseen by elders from the community known as *Chaudhrani*s/*Chaudhry*s, *nayak*s, or *daratni*s. Although the use of the term *gharana* to describe *trans-hijra* relational networks primarily in India appears only very recently in common parlance and publications derived from place-specific ethnographic works (Dutta 2012; Roy 2015a: 10–13), its rise echoes the term's regular use in Hindustani music culture which gained prominence in the 1980s as a means of cultivating a sense of tradition, legitimacy, and identity in the face of swift change in and around the economics of music (Roy 2016: 418). The precise organization of such networks has been debated in literature for several decades. For instance, Cohen discusses "supraregional associations," which link *hijra*s "to other cities across South Asia" (1995: 276), while Reddy discusses the organization of *hijra*s into "seven hijra houses or 'lineages' in India" (2005: 9). In an ethnography conducted in small towns and rural areas of West Bengal, Dutta shows that many of the most visible *hijra*s in the region in the 2000s did not belong to these seven lineages, warning against over-emphasizing lineage-based networks, which "potentially delegitimi[ze] subject-positions that cannot be easily assimilated into coherent identities" (2012: 845). These and other findings reveal not only the complexity of how relational networks move across South Asia, but also the schisms that emerge between the ways lineages are conceptualized, practiced, and discussed by practitioners and scholars in different places.[3] These networks, sometimes joined by ancestral lineages across countries, engage in frequent communication over issues of day-to-day governance on social media networks, along with physical meetings and even border crossings by Indian and Pakistani or Bangladeshi and Indian people. The regular movement between places boundaried by the nation state or not, further reveal the interconnected and fragmented nature of such networks of relations.

Major intra-community milestones known as *jalsa*s—also called *roti chatai*, *gharoli roti*, or *muhurta* (an auspicious moment in time)—are performed for the initiation of a *chela*, the new appointment of senior *guru*s, joining of households, conflict arbitration, or after the passing of a *guru*. These events feature elaborate gift-giving performances demonstrating the status and wealth of particular *dera*s, to which *badhai* is intimately tied. Furthermore, *jalsa*s sometimes feature song and dance items from *badhai* repertoires (see Figure 1), which as Roy shows, allow for the staging of *izzat* and other practices contributing to the socioeconomic and cultural vitality of the *gharana* and greater inter-*gharana* community

FIGURE 1 Guru-nani *preparing to sing "Asha Natoru" ("Don't Break My Hopes") at a* jalsa *celebrating her grand*-chela *Saumya's initiation (left); a Jogappa (with a pretend baby) dances to* badhai *song (middle); and Saumya receives* variyan *(or* vail*) during her final unveiling performance (right), Maharashtra, 2010 (Photos: Jeff Roy; Roy 2015a; 2017).*

(2017: 393). Participants may travel across regional and even state boundaries to attend. Indeed, transnational *hijra-khwaja sira-trans* relationalities cross through the tremulous political rifts of the South Asian region, including the India–Pakistan Partition (1947), the Bangladesh Liberation War (1971), the Kashmir conflict (1947–), and other ensuing conflicts between national, religious, linguistic, and ethnic border zones. They also trace themselves through different legal activist and international non-governmental organization (NGO) funding circulations and networks of communication, which negotiate and sometimes ally with the logics of nation, capital, and identity across the Global North. In this book, we understand all networks of grassroots communication, vernacular but otherwise transnational, to flow across intersecting symbolic, physical, social, and sensorial pathways through the *hijrascape*, drawing from shared understandings and practices specific to *hijra-khwaja sira-trans* worldmaking.

Like the networks from which they emerge, oral histories from *hijra-khwaja sira-trans* lineages engage a plurality of interconnected origin narratives that span religion, language, and geo-political boundaries. While scholarship around *badhai* has often prioritized Hindu myth and ritual, we highlight the many ways different religious referents and oral histories intersect and overlap across boundaries of state and region. There is an abundance of origin narratives that vary across spaces and beliefs, from stories centering Shiva and Arjuna (Hiltebeitel 1980: 151–4; Nanda 1990: 30–2) or Amba/Śikhandin in Hindu myth (Ung Loh 2014), to Islamic narratives of Madina and Mecca, the Umayad Caliphate commander Bin Qasim, Sufi saints, to the Mughal Courts (Pamment 2010; 2019a). Research has shown that some Indian lineages locate mythology in Hindu Mother Goddesses, such as Bahuchara Mata/Bedraj Mata/Murga, who also appears in Bangladeshi narrations as Maya Ji/Tara Moni/Murgawali Ma (Hossain 2021: 112–15).[4] For instance, Roy demonstrates how some *trans-hijra* vocalists in Western Maharashtra and Gujarat call upon Bahuchara Mata to "sing through their voices" in the widely performed cross-regional *badhai* song, "Asha Natoru" ("Don't Break My Hopes"), as demonstrated in the opening vignette to this introduction (Roy 2015a: 189–211; 2016: 417). In Pakistan, performers often call upon Islamic sources, attributing their rights (*haq*) to give blessings to Allah. They may draw on Sufi spiritual associations of the socially disruptive ascetic *faqir* lullaby praising the Prophet's guardian Hazrat Halima, the Shi'a-Sufi dance-prayer of *dhamaal*, and devotional songs to Sufi saints (Pamment 2019a). Such religious repertoires sometimes travel across borders of nation, region, and religion, refusing exclusivity. These convergences speak to *hijra*'s "supra" religious pious practices, in which those who reference Hindu goddesses may participate in Islamic ritual (Hossain 2012: 497–9; Reddy 2005: 100, 117, 120). In many contexts, for instance, it is common for Muslim *guru*s to possess altars with displays of saints and Hindu gods and goddesses, particularly Bahuchara Mata. Some *khwaja sira* and *hijra* people relate that at the battle of Karbala, the men go one way and the women another, and *khwaja siras* are guided by Hazrat Ali, a central figure in Shi'a Islam, who says reassuringly, "Don't worry, you won't be alone, other khwaja siras will come to you from different religions, nations and castes, all growing into one culture" (Gogi 2019). This has parallels with groups who link the power of blessings to Rama, the divine hero of the Ramayana, who before exile gives orders to men and women to depart to their homes; *hijras* patiently wait for years, and as a consequence Rama bestows upon them ritual powers (Reddy 2005: 147). The multiplicity of religious and ritual symbolic referents that inform *hijra-khwaja sira-trans* practices illuminate, among other things, *badhai*'s dexterity across beliefs, temporalities, and spatialities of their publics and of the composition of performers.

Performance, Publics, Reciprocities

Repertoire is passed down through the lineage, though in many cases this follows no fixed sequence, nor do all performance gatherings call for all items. *Badhai*s may begin with an "arrival call," a verbal call down the street praising the householder, followed by singing invoking the goddess (see "Asha Natoru" in Figure 1), Allah's benevolence and/or the assertions of the Sufi *faqir*. Gestural "blessings" for individual celebrants—a gentle touch of the hand to the head, or the rocking of a child—accompany the call and/or may also be performed during opportune moments throughout the performance (see Figure 2). The call is sometimes followed by items that are context-specific and dependent on the occasion, such as the *sehra/shadi* song (wedding song) or *lori/jaccha baccha* (lullaby). These items are often accompanied by a series of *filmi*, devotional, and/or regionally specific songs and dances, along with comic repartee, which all contribute to the occasion and give blessings. Particular repertoires find expression through the skills of individual performers, in negotiation with the collective labor of the group, and through interactions with

FIGURE 2 *A* hijra *blessing a newborn by anointing the head with mustard oil in a* badhai *performance, Dhaka, 2015 (Photo: Adnan Hossain).*

publics. Amidst these relationalities, performance items seep in from other contexts. For instance, performers may showcase their experience of plate dancing from the circus, Sufi and/ or Shi'a devotees may take whirls in a *dhamaal*, an inspired singer may recite a sensual *sher* (poetry), young *chela*s may offer their favorite scandalous Bollywood *filmi* items, or an elder present a classical *kathak* dance item or erotic love song. Publics may also gesture to their item requests. The sonic elements of performance may also emerge from and inform the reciprocal relationship between performer, audience, and space, that constitute *jagah* (place). Here, the embodied crafts of musical creativity, playful ambiguity, versatility, and sonic possibility explore the relations between notes, or "*rag*-spaces" (Neuman 2004: 207), as well as undertake the aesthetic and affective work of building and shaping them through dynamic interplay between bodies and the spaces in which they find themselves (Roy 2017: 403–4).

The groups that perform *badhai* are small intergenerational ensembles (typically three to six members) known as *toli* (literally troupe or band). *Toli*s feature *guru*s and their *chela*s, which may extend to three generations of performers, including *guru-dadi*s/*nani*s or *nan-guru*s (grandparents), their *chela*s who are also *guru*s, and their *chela*s. *Badhai* performers may be selected for already-existing skills and/or may be trained in such roles as playing the *dholak*—also called *dhol* and *dholki* depending on region—or harmonium (manually pumped reed organ, sometimes called *baja* in Punjabi), singing lead parts, or dancing as an integral part of life-learning in the *guru–chela* relationship (Roy 2015a: 28).[5] The *toli* sometimes includes male musicians from outside of immediate *hijra-khwaja sira* communities. In areas of North India and Pakistan, these musicians often belong to different performance lineages known as *mirasi* (lit. custodians of heritage), who similarly deploy knowledge of their publics' family backgrounds inherited from their predecessors (Pamment 2017: 7–8). While positions within the *toli* are generally assigned by the senior *guru*, usually according to flexible hierarchical arrangements that accommodate the specific skills and expertise of individual members, in this collaborative and improvisatory performance practice, roles dovetail and collide. The *guru* who often has more experience invariably navigates the group, cueing different elements of the repertoire, and making demands for *badhai*. The *guru* may also sing, dance, play the *dholak*, partake in comic items, facilitate performances in managerial positions, and/or lead their *chela*s through *badhai* repertoire (see Roy 2015a: 191). *Chela*s who perform may take on leading roles in dancing, singing, and *dholak* playing, and/or secondary positions in the singing (responding in call-and-response numbers), percussion, clapping, or theatrically driven elements. The musical accompaniment typically features the beat of the *dholak*, the *chimta* (tongs), *manjeera* or *sheesha* (metal clappers), harmonium, *ghungroo* worn by a dancer, and the *hijra* "signature clap" (Roy 2015a: 1; Hossain 2021: 74–5; Pamment 2019b). *Chela*s may also take on managerial tasks, such as interacting with patrons and audiences, arbitrating conflicts when they arise between neighbors or within households, monitoring and engaging in local and regional politics, assisting *guru*s with finances, nursing or nurturing elders, and cooking. *Badhai* therefore entails labor across *hijra-khwaja sira-trans* households and in public spaces.

Badhai moves in and through a myriad of physical spaces, from public streets and open grounds to private domestic spaces, as performers cultivate their repertoire and relations with different *dunyadar*, or "people of the world." *Badhai* often occurs in porous spaces that are rarely found in urban infrastructures of elite gated communities, high rise apartments, and other closed structures. The *ilaka*s (areas or territories) in which *badhai* is performed are passed down through the lineage, which marks *virit* or *birit* (territorial divisions) in allocating particular neighborhoods or villages to *toli*s. While territorial disputes may arise between different groups, this arrangement enables *hijra-khwaja sira-trans* performers to craft specialized knowledge on their publics and build relationships across generations of *guru*s and patrons. Indeed, performances draw from and engender the spaces in which they arise. *Badhai*'s often circular or crisscrossing lattice arrangements of performers and audiences enables fluid, improvisatory, participatory, and hybridized genres, offering an interplay of bodies, sounds, and affects. Ideal and profitable spaces for performances invariably offer performers and audiences access and movement, between public and domestic sites. Streets, foyers, and open courtyards of households entail such interstitiality (see Figure 3), enabling performers to draw in both many publics and their celebrant householders, which in turn generates multiplicitous income or gift giving.

While gifts may be given at the end or beginning of some performances, ranging from food stuffs to livestock to cash sums, the showering of cash during these performances,

FIGURE 3 *A* toli *ensemble featuring Maham (center), cueing musicians (foreground), encircled by publics at a* vadhai *performance, Lahore, 2019. Still from the film* Vadhai: A Gift *(Pamment et al. 2019c).*

known as *vail*, is an important part of the intercorporeal event of performance. *Vail*—sometimes called *variyan*—is performed when money is thrown at or encircled over the heads of performers, babies, and audiences, including wedding celebrants, family members or neighbors, and other *hijra-khwaja sira-trans* participants. The performative gesture, which is also found in other South Asian performance contexts such as at weddings and births, requires audiences to play along, and is often a vehicle of playful competition amongst each other as performers and patrons showcase their generosity, status, presence, and/or "preference" for certain performances (Pamment 2017: 11–12; Roy 2015a: 228–230). As Roy shows, *variyan* is frequently featured in *jalsas* and other *trans-hijra* community-based events, and in some cases, is the focus of song lyrics that accompany declarative acts of gift-giving for initiate *chelas* and their *gurus*. Conducted in playful, improvisatory ways, the performance offers possibilities of *izzat* as community members signal their relationalities, wealth, and social status across performers and audiences

within the *gharana* and across the inter-*gharana* community
(2015a: 251–56; 2017: 407). In these and other contexts, the
gesture signals the sacrificial giving of money alongside other
objects of high social value for someone else, the warding
off of the evil eye, and the conveying of blessings. Such
reciprocal interactions between performers and publics, where
getting the audiences to give *badhai* is paramount, prompts
performers to draw material into their repertoire, which push
and pull affective and sensorial thresholds through spectacle,
spiritualities, desires, and deep intimacies. As performers play
with, in, and across a multiplicity of boundaries that have
socially set them apart, *badhai* remains "edgy" to formal
constraints.

Lingering Legacies of the Colonial Gaze

While *hijra-khwaja sira-trans* scholarship has increased
exponentially over the last several decades with the development
of LGBTQIA+ rights movements in South Asia and around the
world, performances by these communities have arguably been
elided. *Badhai* is often glossed over as the "traditional" and/
or "ritual role," suggesting its ahistoricity or presence out of
time and space, rendering it "backwards" or antithetical to the
sometimes intersecting logics of NGO interventions, neoliberal,
and/or religious nationalisms. In the expanding focus on
transgender rights, *badhai* practitioners have sometimes
been accused of extortion and polluting public space, and/or
situated within narratives of decline. The following sections
trace the shifting yet lingering legacy of the colonial visual
regime, through which these practices have often been read
and which invariably explain *away* performance, to advocate
for alternative modes of engagement and imagine alternative
pasts, presents, and futures of *badhai*.

Colonial Surveillance

Until recently, colonial and postcolonial studies on *hijra-khwaja sira-trans* communities predominantly fetishized *hijra* bodily morphology. Criminalizing colonial accounts of *hijra* performance practices literally and symbolically put performers on the surgical operating table (Arondekar 2009: 67–91; Hinchy 2019: 176–88), driven by a panoptic "seeing" of these performers as vehicles of disease and "sexual deviancy." Even before the British period of Crown Rule (1858–1947), various European travelers and officials cast shade on how the *hijra* figure was "openly tolerated" through depictions of performances at a Muslim Eid festival (Burnes 1829)[6] to *hijra*s urinating on houses that refuse *badhai* (Solvyns 1808, in Hinchy 2019: 62), setting the stage for seeing *hijra*s as polluting matter. Denoted by the colonial record as "eunuchs" (often defined as impotent men), *hijra*s were suspected of kidnapping and castrating boys, along with "deviant" sexual practices and "unnatural offences" in collusion with Section 377, the "anti-sodomy" legislation of 1860. In her extended work around the colonial archives, Hinchy explains that to a "British view, the performances and transvestism of hijras posed a threat of moral and sexual contagion to both Indian men and colonial public space" (2014: 276). Like the colonial policing and erasure of courtesans, *devadasi*s, and their dance (Chakravorty 2008; Sachdeva 2008; Soneji 2011; Srinivasan 1985), *hijra-khwaja sira-trans* performances were seen as the vehicles of contagious disease, rather than art. As Hinchy notes, while these performances are rarely elaborated for their actual content, performance is often denigrated by colonial legislators as polluting and "obscene," and even physicians denounce "filthy, obscene, and abusive songs" (2019: 62).

The coupling of performance and sex is pernicious in colonial literatures[7] and anxieties about these performances were at the forefront of anti-*hijra* legislation (enacted in the

NWP and drawn up in the Punjab) of the Criminal Tribes Act (CTA) Pt 2 (1871):

> Any eunuch so registered who appears, dressed or ornamented like a woman [...] or who dances or plays music, or takes part in any public exhibition, in a public street or place or for hire in a private house, may be arrested without warrant.
>
> (in Hinchy 2019: 108)

The emphasis on visual surveillance is a repeated refrain in the CTA legislative debates. For instance, in the prelude to the act, "their movements should be very carefully watched" (Sapte 1865). Later, those who are still singing and dancing should be "narrowly watched" (Hobart 1875), and those who "are strictly watched, [...] have lost their old occupation of dancing and singing in female clothes" (Tyrwhitt 1878, all cited in Pamment et al. 2021: 224). Arondekar elaborates on this panoptic seeing in her reading of the case of Queen Empress vs. Khairati (1884), where Khairati apparently seen "singing dressed as a woman" in a women's gathering was rendered a visible suspect of "being a eunuch" and of "unnatural" sexual acts under Section 377 (2009: 67–91). Arondekar suggests that physical markers (performance, dress, bodily comportment, and "sodomy wounds") provide the lexicon for erasing "the shadow of doubt or ambiguity" haunting the colonial collection of evidence against unnatural practices (2009: 88). This importantly draws attention to the perpetuation of colonial violence in the archival "recovery" of queer, necessitating alternative methodologies.

Despite the powerful presence of visual regimes in the colonial record, which also emerge in some elite Indian "middle class" narratives from the colonial period (Hinchy 2019: 90–2), *hijra* bodies and their performance practices evaded, disrupted, and/or moved beyond these taxonomies in different ways. Governance was uneven and fraught, with colonial administrators frustrated over the elusiveness of bodies they sought to police (Hinchy 2019: 167–93). Further, the colonial record often masks views of publics toward these practices, rendering invisible the relationalities and patronage that probably sustained *badhai* over criminalization regimes (Pamment 2015).[8] Our centering of contemporary performance in this book, while acknowledging the persistence—and shifting—colonial gaze,[9] aligns with what Diana Taylor describes as the mutually constitutive relationship between archive and the repertoire (2003). Through an emphasis on *badhai*'s multiple repertoires, relationalities, aesthetics, affects and sensual possibilities, we "prioritize relational and embodied forms of knowledge production and transmission that take us beyond the colonizing and restrictive epistemic grids" (Taylor 2020: xi). In so doing, we seek to confront how the colonial archive continues to play out "in the formation of cultural institutions, cultural classes and the production of cultural and aesthetic values" (Prakash 2021) through an emphasis on *badhai*'s multiple repertoires, relationalities, aesthetics, affects, and sensorial possibilities.

Ethnographic Assemblages

In recent scholarship on *hijra* communities, colonial regimes continue to linger. The first *hijra*-focused book-length ethnography (Nanda [1990] 1999) presented *hijras* as a pan-Indian "third gender" community—a contested term that offers a tokenized alternative category to western sex/gender dimorphism (Cohen 1995: 277; Dutta 2012: 826; Hossain 2017: 1428–9; Reddy 2005: 4)—organized around the ideal of emasculation rooted in Hindu myth and ritual (Hiltebeitel 1980: 161–5). This practice, Nanda argued, contributed to *hijras*' power to bless or curse in *badhai*, linking "*hijras* to two of the most powerful figures in the Hindu religion, Shiva and the Mother Goddesses, and it is emasculation that sanctions the *hijras*' ritual role as performers at marriages and births"

(1999: 24). Nanda suggests that only asexuality, afforded through castration or *nirban*, and *hijra*s' links to specific Hindu religious figures and ideas, grants authenticity to *badhai* practitioners. The performances are elucidated through such terms as "shameless," "aggressive female sexuality," "grotesque," "sexually suggestive parody," "loud" (1999: 1), "outrageous" and "salacious" (1999: 3)—terms that are strikingly similar to the degradation and downward class/caste views found in the colonial record. Although research has challenged the centrality of emasculation and essentializing religious practices in the production and sanctioning of the *hijra* subject (Cohen 1995; Dutta 2012; Hossain 2012, 2018; Nagar 2020; Reddy 2005), literature has persistently framed *badhai* almost exclusively within Hindu ritual markers (Feinberg 1996: 45; Reddy 2005: 97; Saria 2021: 56–61; Senelick 2000: 25–7). In the context of widespread anti-Muslim and caste violence that has been a mainstay of Modi's Hindu nationalist government (2014–), and rising religious nationalisms across the region, we seek to move beyond essentializing scripts of religion, body morphology, and other markers of legitimacy. In doing so, we highlight *badhai*'s performances of ambiguity within and across a "multiplicity of differences" (Reddy 2005: 186), through the unfolding HIV/AIDS, LGBTQIA+, and liberal rights-based movements, and their neoliberal, nationalist, and religious frameworks.

NGO Interventions

Amidst the rapid rise of HIV/AIDS funding and the proliferation of NGOs, particularly at the turn of the twenty-first century, many gender and sexual minorities, including *hijra*s and other gender nonconforming people, were initially subsumed under the contested category "men who have sex with men" (MSM). *Hijra*s were recast as an "indigenous MSM category, as metonymic figures of 'sexual difference' in compendia of LGBTQIA+ studies on the one hand, and as an integral part of the MSM or *kothi* sexual community on the other," which was actively targeted by government and public health interventions (Reddy 2018: 52), with regional variations.[10] HIV/AIDS funding reached India and Bangladesh in the 1990s, and in the 2010s these nation states began to advance rights recognitions for *hijra* people beginning with Bangladesh in 2013 (see Figure 4) and followed by India in 2014. Due to economic sanctions placed on Pakistan in the 1990s, HIV/AIDS funding arrived later in the country (Qureshi 2018: 39), while *khwaja sira* rights were taken up by its Supreme Court in 2009, earlier than India and Bangladesh, a move which called NGOs and the government to take action toward social rehabilitation.

Throughout South Asia, the absorption of *hijra* identities under the MSM umbrella unsettled their status as celebate or

FIGURE 4 *A drama performance on raising community awareness about HIV/AIDS in an NGO in Dhaka, 2010 (Photo: Adnan Hossain).*

asexual—a status sometimes claimed to be important to *hijra* authentication amongst some *badhai* performers themselves, as Nanda and Reddy signal above. Such projections of asexuality might be read as strategies of survival, considering that *hijra*s were marked as sexually deviant and criminal under the colonial-era anti-sodomy Section 377, which continues to be legally inscribed in Bangladesh and Pakistan.[11] Some *hijra-khwaja sira-trans* people tried to distance themselves from HIV/AIDS interventions, avail them secretly, or circumvent the discourse around sexuality (Khan 2014). The emergence of "transgender" in public discourse and new social movements that privileged legal, rights-based language and activism, marked a distinction from MSM, "forg[ing] a bifurcated schema of identification such that the government, funders, and NGOs increasingly distinguish between transgender and same-sex desiring persons not just as distinct individual identities, but also as segregated populations" (Dutta 2013: 497). As Reddy notes:

> at this time, the transgender community, while still made up largely of *hijra*s, was also expanding to include transmen as well as transwomen who did not necessarily identify as *hijra*s, even as reductive semantic framings continued to manifest themselves, truncating the gender, embodied, and linguistic variance of the trans-feminine category, as well as playing into existing tropes of authenticity, and excluding transmen from its purview—exclusions and reductive usages that linger to this day.
>
> (2018: 53)

Even as Global North taxonomies of identity disseminated, their significations acquired place-based orientations, playing out differently in relation to a range of vernacular identities, religions, local activist, and solidarity movements, economic policy, and political borders of postcolonial nationhood.

Rights, Neoliberal, and Religious Nationalisms

Reanimating some of the violence of the colonial record, legislative discussions around *hijra-khwaja sira-trans* rights point to the contested role of *badhai* performance and kinship practices in nationalist and transnational scripts of rights-based movements. Rights movements have sometimes focused on making *hijra-khwaja sira* people into "useful citizens," co-opted *badhai* in employment quotas of *hijra-khwaja sira* tax collectors or traffic wardens, or demonized it as anathema to the service of national interests. In India, the acknowledgement of a "rich cultural tradition" comprising performances formed part of the argument produced by Anand Grover to the Indian Supreme Court, which paved the way for 2014 rights legislation (Roy 2016: 416) while NGOs, politicians, and prominent *trans-hijra* leaders continue to admonish the practice of *badhai*. In Pakistan, performance arguably fueled legislative hearings against the human rights violations inflicted upon these communities in 2009, following *guru* Almas Bobby's protest with over a hundred *khwaja sira* people at the Taxila police station after the arrests and abuse of *khwaja sira* dancers performing at a wedding party (Pamment 2019a). Nevertheless, legal debates quickly turned to denounce performance and the kinships that cultivate them. Promoting a politics of respectability, morality, and normative citizenship, the Chief Justice described interventions that would make *khwaja sira* people into "good citizens" (Pamment 2019a: 298), and called on collaboration from NGOs and civil society toward their "social rehabilitation." In Bangladesh, the route to recognition and legitimation of *hijra*s as worthy subjects of social development followed a non-judiciary path, where a government policy decision declared them as a legal category of gender/sex in 2013 (Hossain 2017). Like elsewhere in South Asia, subsequent state policies and strategy papers have explicitly referenced *badhai* performance as a "backward communitarian practice" that interferes with *hijra*s' social empowerment, and therefore in need of eradication through various livelihood programs to refashion and mainstream *hijra*s into "respectable citizens."

In the legal terrain of rights, the employment of the "good/ bad" citizen binary has had particular ramifications for *cholla* (variant *challa*) or *dheenga* (in areas of Pakistan), the collection of alms or monies and foodstuffs from the marketplaces, or other public sites, along with other community practices across South Asia. For instance, Pakistan's 2018 Transgender Persons (Protection of Rights) Act remains explicitly punitive about begging (Pamment forthcoming b; Redding 2019). The 2016 version of the Indian Transgender bill contained explicit provisions against "begging," while the 2019 version of the bill has replaced explicit mention of the term with "forced or bonded labor," which may nonetheless continue to criminalize the practice indirectly (Dutta et al. 2022). Contravening long-running cultural logics of reciprocity and gift exchange that inform the public reception and engagement with *hijra*s, *badhai* and *cholla* are now construed in Bangladeshi popular media and everyday middle-class discourses not only as forms of extortion but also public nuisance (Hossain 2021). In this book, we position *badhai* and *cholla* as interconnected, whose contested boundaries sometimes fluidly overlap in kinship practices and engagements with publics.

The demarcations of legitimate citizenship have intersected with neoliberal globalization, driving new economies and practices of performance. These are exemplified by media campaigns facilitated by NGOs, prominent figures, and corporate sponsors, which emphasize "economic freedom," upward mobility, and a politics of respectability. In India, Roy shows how "India's first professional trans-led ensemble" known as the Dancing Queens (deemed a "modern-day *gharana*") have staged their performances with media production support made possible by NGO, corporate, and various media collaborators. The centering of pan-Indian regional dance forms (excluding *badhai*) and theatrical numbers centering successful "coming out" narratives detailing economic independence (from the *dera*) appear to evince the transformation of regimes and representations of *hijra* identity from "devalorized codes of social difference to respectable, middle-class ones [promoting a] narrative of self-understanding and personal empowerment," encoded in a language of neoliberal nationalism (Roy 2019a: 181). Other viral media campaigns produced by different local media outlets include a campaign depicting eighteen trans men and women holding placards stating "I am Not a Hijra" (Mount 2020; Sengupta 2017) and another depicting *hijra* people singing India's national anthem while dressed as middle-class workers (Hindustan Times 2015). These NGO supported projects have been critiqued for drawing a line between *trans* and *hijra* communities, reinforcing a politics of respectability, foreclosing other possibilities of being through a "template of nationalism" (India TV 2015; MissMalini 2015; NDTV 2015; Bhattacharya 2019: 2). In the Pakistani context, Pamment shows how the *hijra* clap, a potent performance of *hijra* identity and resistance, is figured as a stigmatizing and "backward" gesture in #ChangeTheClap (2017), a Pakistani social media human rights campaign on behalf of the international NGO Asia Pacific Transgender Network (APTN) donor (2019b). The campaign presents "street *khwaja siras*" collecting alms and occupying public space as victims, in favor of "positive representations" of transwomen on a five-star hotel fashion ramp, and transmen and transwomen in NGO sectors and education institutions—suggesting that those who do not conform to such images are responsible for the violence inflicted upon them. Indeed, similar movements are emerging from Bangladesh, where the recent appearance of transwomen as a new category of respectable middle-class trans-femininity works to undermine and marginalize *hijra* identity as incompatible with the new nationalist agenda of social development and neoliberal trans empowerment. The popular proclivity to conscript and celebrate a few individual stories of successful assimilation into the mainstream, for example Tashnuva Anan Shishir's recent debut as the first transgender news anchor in Bangladesh (BBC 2021) or Hochemin Islam's funded studentship in a university public health program (Antara 2021), deflects attention from the structural and systemic gender, sexuality, and class-based hierarchies and injustices that many *hijras* often experience. Such exclusionary logics are also evident in the mainstream performance spaces across South Asia to which *hijra-khwaja sira-trans* identified performers are routinely denied access.

Recent calls for religious nationalism across South Asia have exacerbated existing social hierarchies within and across the *hijrascape*. In India, notable figures like Laxmi Narayan Tripathi—who in 2015 participated in the formation of the Akhil Bharatiya Kinnar Akhada, a Hindu monastic order for *kinnar*s (a contested, Sanskritized word for *hijra*)—have been critiqued for appeals to ethno-nationalism, anti-Pakistani rhetoric, and bolstering Hindutva ideology (Bhattacharya 2019; TNM 2018; Upadhyay 2020), while giving speeches alluding to *badhai*'s abolishment. Such actions exploit caste, class, and religious privileges within *trans-hijra* communities across the country, pushing non-upper caste and Muslim individuals and *gharana*s further to the peripheries of power and influence. Other movements across the country are working to fortify the communities' ties to Hinduism. In Tamil Nadu, for instance, *thirunangai* (literally, "respectable woman") communities have been "incorporated as a vital constituency of devotees" in significant ways at Kuthandavar-Aravan, or Koovagam, through their roles in the re-enactment of Mohini's wedding to Kuthandavar, or Aravan, from the Mahabharata epic (Hiltebeitel 1995; Vasudevan 2020: 15).[12] Koovagam has become a contested site for advancement of state-sanctioned visibility through NGO-sponsored community events, while the recasting of *trans-thirunangai* people as emissaries of Hindu heritage "enacts further constrictions, particularly for Muslim and Christian people, as [such] communities continue to navigate, adapt to, resist, and/or challenge forces of post/colonial modernity" (Roy forthcoming). In Bangladesh, there has been a recent rise of interest among *ulema*s in the Islamic position on *hijra*s, which include the setting up of a new *madrassa* (religious seminary) exclusively for *hijra*s (Chowdhury 2020) and an Islamic militant group has also been targeting *hijra*s as potential recruits to further their ideological mission (Porosh 2021). However, the Islamic position on *hijra*s is as variegated as these communities, as Hossain contends elsewhere (2012). In Pakistan, the rising visibility of *khwaja sira* people engaged with the transnational Islamic Deobandi-inflected missionary movement, the Tablighi Jama'at, has seen some *khwaja sira tablighi*s renounce performance, while some *tablighi*s are coupling preaching with dancing (Pamment forthcoming a). Further, a newly opened "Church for Eunuchs" in Karachi (Gannon 2020), alongside a rise of *khwaja sira madrassa*s, evidence some parallels with *badhai*'s "supra" religious practices. As Pamment argues, the many religious spaces and doings that continue to offer *khwaja sira* people worldmaking possibilities—"challenge unilinear futures of religious orthodoxy" (forthcoming a). All of these shifting vectors indicate a spectrum of possibilities and challenges for *badhai* practitioners across the *hijrascape*.

Continued Contestations

Amidst the worldwide Covid-19 epidemic, *hijra-khwaja sira-trans* people across South Asia have become further vulnerable as already-precarious and marginalized subjects of nation states. As we write this book collectively in the midst of quarantine, we have become sensitive to the growing awareness of the particularities of *hijra-khwaja sira-trans* precarity in this time, which in some contexts has entailed the suspension of *badhai* and other practices of livelihood, increasing debt in a bid to survive the lockdown (Hossain and Esthappan 2021), and an increase of physical and symbolic violence in domestic, private, and public spaces. In Bangladesh, for instance, many *hijra*s have been evicted from their homes, due largely to inflexible rent policy, pushing many onto the streets without access to health care, and struggling for livelihood in the face of economic recessions and stigma. The country's general public have labeled unhoused *hijra*s as "active agents" and "carriers of the coronavirus" (Hossain 2022); like the colonial record, they are regarded as vehicles of contagion, pollution, or defilement. While acknowledging such struggles, we maintain a critical position on the overwhelming linear narrative that situates *badhai* on the decline, considering that such discourses have played significant roles to disenfranchise *hijra-khwaja sira-trans* performers across South Asia. The social reception of these performances has always been ambiguous—even in the colonial period—pointing to *badhai*'s continued elusivity, multiplicity, resistance to classificatory schemes and taxonomies, and capacities for adaptation amidst numerous contestations.

Although state-sanctioned practices and policies have paved the way for the visibilization of *hijra-khwaja sira-trans* communities throughout South Asia—which has indeed raised awareness about *hijra-khwaja sira-trans* plight— visibility as a precondition to social reform and wellbeing also "risks erasing the fluidity and multivocality that are integral" to the lives and practices that make up these communities, as Craddock references in their work with *thirunangai* communities in Tamil Nadu (Craddock 2018; Vasudevan 2020). As Reddy notes, the recognition of community rights to existence without providing mechanisms to redistribute power merely expands the reach of the state, forcing minority communities to reinscribe their marginality to claim entitlements, reifying pre-existing hierarchies of status and authenticity in the process (2018). As we show above, *badhai* and other *hijra-khwaja sira-trans* cultural practices arguably fall through the cracks in the process of claiming identity and legitimacy, risking invisibilization on the performance floor (Roy 2016; 2019a), further marginalization in mainstream spheres of political policy and discourse (Pamment 2019a), and overall "decline." In this book, we wish to follow *badhai* through the fissures produced by these post/colonial projects not to shine a light on them for the purposes of classification, codification, or territorialization, but to explore what such absences may bring to *hijra-khwaja sira-trans* studies or studies of performance more broadly. Our work in this book and elsewhere reveals some of the different ways *hijra-khwaja sira-trans* performers have responded to these—and indeed other—challenges, whether adopting "strategic essentialist" approaches to claim authenticity along religious or ethnic-nationalist lines, launching their performances into new social spaces for "respectable" middle-class audiences (Roy 2016; 2019a), or disrupting such forces altogether through entirely different means (Pamment 2019a; forthcoming a; Roy forthcoming).

Interventions

Dwight Conquergood draws on de Certeau's aphorism "'what the map cuts up, the story cuts across'" to advocate "transgressive travel between two different domains of knowledge: one official, objective, and abstract—'the map'; the other one practical, embodied and popular—'the story.' This promiscuous traffic between different ways of knowing carries the most radical promise of performance studies research" (2002: 145). In this book we seek to untether the study of *badhai* from its colonial and postcolonial mappings, foreclosed by ocularcentrism, biopolitics, the nation state, and codified regimes of the performing arts. We instead open *badhai* to movement—in and across different ways of knowing through our collaborations, with practitioners and as scholars working through different embodied locations, inscribed by geographies, disciplines, and epistemologies. Kasmani describes affective worldmaking as "a moving—insofar as futures and histories, new and other than those given in the social location circumscribed by traditional structures, come to be propelled, pursued, and possibly realized" (2021a: 97). In foregrounding *badhai*'s affective worldmaking, we here describe our various movings, from methodological nationalisms to *hijrascapes*, disciplinary codifications to abundance, and the boundaried authorial self to collaborative authorship.

From Methodological Nationalisms to *Hijrascapes*

Prompted by the "transnational" and "mobility turn" in the social sciences and humanities in the wake of globalization, we seek to challenge hegemonic epistemologies and methodologies of *hijra-khwaja sira-trans* study. While such turns in scholarship have typically focused on the flows of developmentalist discourse, legal reforms, and NGO capital trafficked from or through the Global North (Billard and Nesfield 2021; Dutta 2013; Dutta and Roy 2014; Dutta, et al. 2022; Hossain and Nanda 2020), *badhai* points to a longer history of exchange—including the diffusion of ideas and material goods—across South Asia's changing borders, predating the contemporary manifestations of globalization. Consequently, we turn from India-centered "methodological nationalism" (Hossain 2018; Wimmer and Schiller 2003), that has territorialized dominant scholarly readings of gender and sexuality in South Asia. This involves engaging in acts of collaboration—inspired by a wealth of literatures, conferences, and symposia that have come before—in which our collective work does the necessary labor of drawing across disciplines of study, authorships, geographical regions, and bodies of knowledge (Arondekar et al. 2015; Boellstorff et al. 2014; Puar 2012; Roy 2018; Roy et al. forthcoming; Vikram 2019). While we assume a deterritorialized stance with respect to the study of *badhai*, or the "workings of imagination" that seek to illustrate such an elusive and slippery subject (Appadurai 1996), we also recognize the labor and "pain of the deterritorialized" (Visweswaran 1994: 109) as *hijra-khwaja sira-trans* people are often forced out of natal households, made to travel to find new networks of kinship, learn new languages, convert to new religions, and/or fend for themselves at a young age. Our approach therefore is not to treat *badhai* as a mere disembodied liminal marker of aesthetics but to pay attention to the *hijra-khwaja sira-trans* bodies that render *badhai* possible, the pains and pleasures associated with those bodies and their materialities. We view materialities not only in the sense of embodied subjectivities but also in terms of political economies and unequal access to various resources shaping *hijra-khwaja sira-trans* relationalities.

These interventions are particularly important at this socio-historical juncture not only because of the continued spatio-intellectual dominance of India within South Asia and its studies but also because of the rising authoritarianism across the region that seeks to both reinscribe virulent nationalism and "reterritorialize" cultures and nation-states. Neoliberal globalization, despite its professed claims at loosening the strictures of conventional social and political organization, has had the paradoxical effect of reigniting and reinforcing various ethno-nationalist parochialisms, religious orthodoxies, and colonialisms. The conscripting and recasting of *hijra*s as emblems of a tolerant Hindu Indic heritage by certain political formations in India is just one example of such parochialism that contravenes the long histories of religious pluralism enacted by *hijra-khwaja sira-trans* communities. This collaborative book project seeks to challenge these and other provincial tendencies to reify and appropriate *hijra-khwaja sira-trans* people and cultures. We highlight a multiplicity of *hijra-khwaja sira-trans* subjectivities while bringing into view Muslim—and indeed other interconnected practices—that have had an important hand in forming transnational networks of relationality within and between all three South Asian countries. In doing so, we acknowledge the inevitable incompleteness of our project in not covering *hijra* worldmaking in "all" of South Asia—including (but not limited to) Nepal, Myanmar, and Sri Lanka—nor in its diasporic reach. We also acknowledge the limitations we present in centering almost exclusively urban locations within Bangladesh, India, and Pakistan (see Dutta 2012; Saria 2021, and others for *hijra* studies in rural areas). Although we do not offer substantial deconstruction of the geopolitical imperatives of "South Asia" (Tripathi and Chaturvedi 2020), we remain mindful of Arondekar and Patel's critique of dominant proclivities in queer—and indeed other—scholarships that draw from non-European sources yet remain theoretically underpinned by "US mappings of queer, rather than transacting across questions from different sites, colluding and colliding along the way" (2016: 151). While recognizing the difficulties and conflicts that may arise in doing so in practice, our adoption of a transregional approach allows us to analyze such collusions and collisions, in addressing the "intra-regional effacements and inequalities" (Hossain 2018) across South Asian queer and trans studies.

Hijrascapes enable us to speak to the multi-layered and multi-directional movements and flows that inform the way *hijra-khwaja sira-trans* people craft their own lives within and across different cultures and societies. The suffix *-scape* allows us to examine the fluid, irregular shapes and disjunctures of these landscapes, as well as the profoundly subjective nature of such constructs, which are inflected by the historical, linguistic, and political positionings and orientations of different actors—nation-states, multinationals, diasporic communities, subnational groupings and movements (whether religious, political, or economic), *and* intimate face-to-face groups, such as villages, neighborhoods, and families. These landscapes are the building blocks of what (extending Benedict Anderson 1983) Appadurai designates "imagined worlds," that is, the multiple worlds that are constituted by the historically situated imaginations of persons and groups spread around the globe (Appadurai 1996: 36).

While we draw inspiration from Appadurai to employ *hijrascapes* as an interpretive framework, we do not show any theoretical allegiance to his original formulation of "scapes" thinking. Rather, we mobilize *hijrascapes* as a way to point towards various flows of people, relationalities, ideas, materials, sensorial orientations, and embodiments across many centuries of large-scale interactions in South Asia, as well as the scales of material and symbolic relations within and through which *hijra-khwaja sira-trans* lives are experienced in particular locales. Importantly, working through *hijrascapes* directs our attention to the way people navigate, negotiate, evade, or destabilize boundaries of nation, region, religion, class, caste, ethnicity, language, gender, and sexuality. The idea is not to romanticize a transregional pan South Asian *hijra-khwaja sira-trans* subject position of "culturally interlocked domains" (Peletz 2006) or stable community networks. Instead, *hijrascapes* foreground the uneven movements of inter-, intra-, and sub-regional comings and goings through which *hijra-khwaja sira-trans* relationalities are formed across translocal spatialities (Hossain 2018), of which *badhai* is part. *Hijrascapes* prevent us from reading *badhai* through a timeless "ethnographic present" while alerting us to the way its practitioners in specific times and places negotiate past and present contexts, construct genealogies, and envision futurities.

From Disciplinary Codifications to Abundance

Turning to *badhai*'s many doings, we lean into *and* depart from the performative turn of *hijra* studies, arguably in pivot in the mid-1990s. Kira Hall's work on queer linguistics in Banaras locates agency in *hijra* cultivation of gestures, such as the clap, an "important index of identity" that resists assimilation into normative gender binary embodied doings (in Zimman and Hall 2010: 175), and the coded language or *hijralect*—known as Ulti in Bangladesh and Farsi in parts of North India and Pakistan—"in resistance to systematic exclusion" (Hall 1997: 431). Just as Judith Butler's contributions to gender performativity (1988, and others) have been critiqued for foregrounding performativity over performance (Meyer 2010: 3), in-depth studies of material performances, their myriad of expressions, sensorialities, repertoires, relationalities, temporalities, and spatialities, have often been elided in earlier scholarship.

Overlooking the worlds of performance and/or focusing exclusively on their othering to the codifications of music, dance, and theater as they appear in the classist and/or "classical" projects carries residues of colonial denigration. Such projects exemplify what Roy terms "the exclusionary framings of virtuosity" that delineate "legitimate" performance in scholarly studies and pedagogies (2019b). At the same time, too often are gaps in knowledge represented as failures of analytical skill or training, to be filled and overcome in the interest of producing better, fuller knowledge (Ellawala and Roy 2021). In her work on queer South Asian histories, Arondekar delivers an important critique of the archival recuperative impulse that invariably operates through "a search and rescue model," urging instead epistemological movement "beyond the grammars of failure of loss and toward an archival poetics of ordinary surplus" or "abundance" (2021; 2023). Keeping in mind the historical, phobic impulse to narrate queer- and trans-ness as lacunae, we turn our attention to the ways *hijra-khwaja sira–trans* performers speak, gesture, and sound out in and through the unstable, interstitial spaces between discipline and genre.

The violence of aesthetic legibility and validation is often tied to nationalist projects, and shows up in positivist disciplinary formations of value and worth, or what dance scholar Marta Elena Savigliano calls "aestheticized biopolitics" (2009: 166). As Prasad and Roy have shown, the idea of legitimacy as a performance of virtuosity—aspects of Indian classical music projects which have framed the parameters of performance-based study—"is entwined with compulsory heteropatriarchy and class hierarchies" (2017: 201). This is evidenced by the continued marginalization, erasure, or othering of non-dominant South Asian performances and/or the disembodiment of practitioners from performance practices that challenge or evade the interests of the nation-state. Brahma Prakash critiques the dissociation of "culture" from labor in post-colonial contexts, in which "cultural performance ends up becoming somebody's other: the classical other, the colonial other, post-colonial other, modern and contemporary other, or the middle class's other. Its aesthetic is analysed in the language and terms of the dominant and with imposed theatrical and aesthetic perspectives" (2019: 94). As Prakash and several scholars have argued of Indian nationalist theater projects, such as the Indian People's Theatre Association (IPTA, 1943–67) and the "theatre of roots" (late 1950s–), the artistic and aesthetic value of "folk performances" have often been capitalized and sanitized in the name of "tradition" and "authenticity" by state organizations and elites, invariably maligning their performing laboring bodies. As Rustom Bharucha explains, cultural elites conceived the "folk" as a static and empty "vessel" of the past to be "filled," cleansed, and rescued with new ideas and political content, in the language and terms of the dominant (1993: 198)—exclusions that have permeated theatrical "uses" of the "folk" in Pakistan (Pamment 2017) and Bangladesh (Jamil Ahmed 2014). Prakash suggests such continued puritanical interventions to material contexts of folk performance genres, seek control over an "aesthetics of defilement" (2019: 151). He elaborates such aesthetics through *launda nach/bidesia* of Bihar, as the tenacity to "contaminate and corrupt purity of forms by mixing, bringing and polluting them together" (151; see also Dutta forthcoming). Parallel treatments accompany the South Indian hereditary dancers known as *devadasi*s through the centering of respectable middle-class, Brahmin bodies on the dance stage (Gaston 1996; Kamath 2019; Kersenboom 1995, 1987; Soneji 2011); the sanitization of female voices in the recording studio (Weidman 2006); the fetishization and white-washing of women in trans/national Indian dance (Putcha forthcoming); the erasure of the surveillance and intervention on performing Odissi dancers (Banerji 2010); the exoticization and sidelining of *tawaif* and *baiji* performers

(Chakravorty 2008); the stigma leveled at women artists of the Tamil stage (Seizer 2005); the arrests of Punjabi women stage dancers in Pakistan (Pamment 2012); the crackdown on *kothi* dancers, bar dancers, and "illicit" performance forms through laws and along Indian nationalist moral codes of respectability (Morcom 2014; Puri 2016); the erasure of Tamil Islamic—and indeed other—influences in the creation of the region's *raga*-based music (Soneji forthcoming); the erasure of Muslim musicians and communities of exponents of instruments like the *sarangi* and *sarod,* in the Hindustani music world (Bor 1986–7; Katz 2017; Neuman 1990; Qureshi 2007). Rather than measuring *badhai* through the language of dominant aesthetics, we understand *badhai* to draw from many inspirations—including but not limited to music and sound, dance and/or theater, the dominant or "classical"— often disrupting and remaking the contours of the genres and sources from which such inspirations arise in "imperfect-yet-sincere" and participatory ways (Prasad and Roy 2017: 195).

Perhaps part of *badhai*'s perceived disciplinary illegibility— at least insofar as studies of music, dance, theater, and anthropology are concerned—lies in its capacity to borrow from and recycle itself with other performance forms and genres, challenging norms of originality, expertise, and authenticity as implicit yet necessary preconditions to valid disciplinary study (Prasad and Roy 2017). In turn, *badhai* lends disruptive possibilities to Euro-centric, cisheteropatriarchal sensorial boundaries and hierarchies of knowledge that have typically animated studies on sound, affect, and performance. Recycling is a useful heuristic to engage with the hybrid, heterogeneous, shifting, and expansive repertoires of *badhai*. Marvin Carlson describes recycling as critical to theater's complex play with cultural memory: "the present experience is always ghosted by previous experiences and associations while these ghosts are simultaneously shifted and modified by the process of recycling and recollection" (2001: 2). While Carlson gravitates to recyclings of dramatic text, body, stage, and play house— *badhai* opens up more capacious recyclings: rituals, gestures, choreographies, musics, sounds, spaces, ad infinitum. The conceptual terrain of "repetition with a difference," a hallmark of performance studies' "restored behavior" (Schechner 1985)—lends some resonance to *badhai*'s "impure" recyclings, of folk genres entailing an "aesthetics of defilement," (Prakash 2019) particularly in the contexts of state interests, classist, casteist, and heteronormative imperatives.

While performance studies offers the authors of this book some shared orientations across disciplines of anthropology, theater, music and sound studies, and queer studies, our approach is interested less in the joining (and expansionism) of our disciplines, and more in their deconstruction. As Arondekar explains, "interdisciplinarity is the mantra that has been summoned to ease the stress of minoritizing practices" characterizing the gaps between disciplines, but when interdisciplinarity gets translated across queer and area studies, we must concern ourselves more with the "breaking down of disciplinary forms" (2021). Edward Said shows how the division and differentiation of ways of knowing is the function of empire (1978), or more succinctly, "discipline is empire" (McKittrick 2021: 38). Our collaboration illuminates some of the violence produced by such disciplines—particularly the structuralist and extractivist impulses of anthropology, ethnomusicology, and other fields—to challenge the "genealogies, legacies, assumptions, and categories of knowledge that define the boundaries of music and other performance studies" (Bacchetta 2010: 153; in Roy 2021: 9) and facilitate the liberation of *badhai* study.

Mindful of the tendencies that emerge through citational practice (Ahmed 2013), we draw inspiration from a growing body of South Asian scholarship that examines performance—including its histories, aesthetics, sensibilities, sensorial and affective possibilities—across the intersections of nationalism (Menon 2013), transnationalism (Medhuri 2008; Srinivasan 2012), piety (Cooper 2021), surveillance and militarism (Banerji 2010; Rashid 2020), feminisms (Lieder 2018; Shroff 2020), trans and queer theories (Gopinath 2018; Kasmani 2017; Khubchandani 2020), and performance methodologies

(Prasad 2020a, 2020b; Putcha forthcoming). Such studies propel our movements out of narrowly conceived disciplinary framings, toward *badhai*'s relationalities and plurality of doings. They also guide our movements as we "interrogate and critique, rather than reproduce or valorize" performance's migrations, tracing the movement of bodies and performances within and across boundaries of nation, knowledge, and the senses (Prasad and Roy 2017: 199). *Badhai*'s constrictions by colonial visual regulatory regimes prompt us to examine the affective and sensorial possibilities such performance brings. Through these reorientations (Ahmed 2006), *badhai* offers new possibilities for laboring collaboratively, and this practice draws our attention to what it does for the people involved in their production and for all of us epistemologically. Such a shift requires intercorporeal engagement with *badhai,* a movement toward coavelness (Fabian 1983) and "co-performative witnessing" through the "labor of reflexivity" (Conquergood 2002; Madison 2007; 2011), an accounting for our bodies in our field sites and in our writing together.

Collaborative Authorship

As we work collectively across the span of three different continents, disciplines, and epistemological borders, our collaboratively authored book seeks to destabilize the "boundaried authorial self," towards the "transparency, transmission, [and] transit" of knowledge production (APWG 2016: 35). In doing so, we offer our individual and collective insights to examine what collisions and alignments emerge with respect to our particular orientations and areas of study in and around *hijra-khwaja sira-trans* performance. Through transgressions of territorialized knowledge, we question the origins and ownership of certain knowledges, as understood and practiced within the context of the neoliberal institution. We also question the completeness of such knowledge to emphasize the always transitory and unfinished qualities of knowledge as it is translated and circulated between, across, within, and outside of our bodies in disparate places. As Visweswaran notes, "ethnography, like fiction, no matter its pretense to present a self-contained narrative or cultural whole, remains incomplete and detached from the realms to which it points" (1994: 1). This becomes all the more complex as we work together in the writing of a book. As ethnographic collaboration expands possibilities of connection—relations we form with people, concepts, theories, and places—so too does it magnify the potential for disconnection or detachment from the very people, concepts, theories, or places before which may have previously been understood as unwavering. In the collaborative search for ethnographic research-driven truths in the "made" world, we understand our fragmented yet intersecting roles in the envisioning and co-creation of new existing or possible worlds.

Anand Pandian asks, "what would it take to nurture an anthropology founded on receptivity to difference—the inevitability, indeed, of wandering, of getting lost—rather than its mastery?" (2019: 8). We enact such wanderings in our collaborative writing. Intersecting through the differences that we each bring, we work together against positivist framings of *badhai,* which entails its "mastery" and "finality." What Sara Ahmed describes plainly as a "turning away from the straight path," we follow *badhai*'s trajectories through neighborhoods and other spaces, recentering performance and its relations that characterize *hijra-khwaja sira-trans* experiences. Through this work, we join/come from a growing community whose work centers queer and trans epistemologies and methodologies in/of South Asia—a chosen family of scholars and practitioners who find joy in experiences and experiential examinations of queer and trans kinships, embodiments, performances, intimacies, agencies, collective actions, justice, and mutual support. Much like the discussions, publications, and artistic works that have emerged in this burgeoning field, the wandering in this book is premised on hope—not to be confused with romanticism—namely, "the hope that those who wander away from the paths they are supposed to follow leave their footprints behind" (Ahmed 2014: 21). The following chapters reveal possible alignments and divergences across the *hijrascape*, which trace the positional, theoretical, and methodological leanings of the authors, as well as the many place-based features and circumstances surrounding *badhai* repertoire, social networks, and practices.

Hossain's "*Badhai* as Dis/ability: Meaning, Context, and Community in Bangladesh" examines the impact of state legislative reform and neoliberal developmentalist initiatives (2013–) upon *badhai* performance in Dhaka. *Hijra*s have been positioned as sexually, genitally, and hormonally *protibondhi* ("handicapped" or "disabled"), in need of rescue and social protection. Such discursive moves have framed the interrelated activities of *badhai* and *cholla* (collection of monies and foodstuffs from marketplaces) as criminally-oriented and polluting extortion, obstacles to social empowerment, reaffirming "real/fake" *hijra* dichotomies. The ongoing postcolonial societal and state vilification of *hijra* performances animates the lingering legacy of colonial violence. Re-figuring *badhai* as ability, Hossain examines these tensions upon the daily routines of several performance groups and their own imagings of *badhai*'s pasts and futures, towards alternative worldmaking.

Pamment's chapter "Shifting Orientations: *Vadhai* in Pakistan" strays away from structuralist framings by foregrounding the affective possibilities of *vadhai* songs, dances, prayers, comedy, gesture, touch, and spectacle, in navigating the immediate and always shifting entanglements of gender, class, religion, sexuality, and kinship. Walking with various ensembles in Lahore, across relationalities between performers, lineages, and *ilaka* audiences, Pamment highlights the intercorporeality of these improvisatory

Punjabi performance repertoires that bring publics to movement—generosity, tears, laughter, into dance, or elsewhere—reorienting, however temporally, hierarchical social arrangements. Following *vadhai*'s entrance into newer national "territories" animated by transgender rights politics (2009–), the chapter unfolds a spectrum of affects as some practitioners play into and/or shift classist, religious, and/ or neoliberal nationalist sentiments. In these multiplicitous registers, affects, movings, and doings, Pamment evidences a dynamic *hijrascape* in Pakistan as performers weave through, spin out, and make loose ends of multiscalar marginalizations.

Roy's chapter "Movements through *Badhai* Sonic Arrangements in India" examines the affective, sensorial, and political possibilities of *badhai* sounds, troubling fixed orientations and habits of writing informed by the colonial gaze through "sincerely queer listening." Cruising through Kanpur, Lucknow, and New Delhi's sonic landscapes, alongside a predominantly Muslim *hijra gharana*, Roy shows how *badhai*s respond to the sensorial ordering of place-based sonic inputs, transforming the rhythms and rhymes of the neighborhood to create parallel, alterior possibilities of being and belonging. Revisiting Roy's previous work in filmmaking (2011, 2011–12, 2015c) the chapter explores what flexible, relational, and multisensorial listening offers through movements of narration, traversing fragmented memories, histories, and intimacies across *ilaka*s, *dera*s, and contested political spaces. Such movements reveal the fleeting and ephemeral interplay of *badhai*'s sonic *mise-en-scène*—or "the heterogeneously constituted, always unfolding possibility of arrangement"—animated by interactions between people, music repertoires, and atmospheres within which they arise and come to pass (Kasmani 2017).

Our different approaches, emplacements, and voices attest to *badhai*'s capacity to be and do multiple things. *Badhai*'s polyvocality constitutes its resistance and survival in the face of post/colonial erasure across shifting *hijrascapes*.

1

Badhai as Dis/Ability: Meaning, Context, and Community in Bangladesh

Adnan Hossain

"Performance is hard work. In the past, *hijra*s like us used to be summoned to sing, dance, and confer blessings on the newborn but these days, even if we sit for hours in front of the door, the households show us no humanity nor do they pay us. Such is the time we are in and all these new state livelihood initiatives and the so-called legal recognition have combined to undermine our livelihoods." Srabonti,[1] a *hijra guru* who I had known for over a decade made the above remark on our way back to their *dera* after a *badhai* performance in a working-class neighborhood of Dhaka in December 2019. I begin this chapter with this quote to highlight the impact of legislative reform and developmentalist initiatives on *badhai* performance in Bangladesh. It turns to a resurgent interest in *hijra*s as a new subject of social development in the wake of their legal recognition as a distinct sex/gender in 2013.[2] It focuses on the way *badhai* performance is being undermined in the face of increasingly reluctant patrons and state-manufactured discourses that vilify and demonize the *hijra*s as criminally oriented abject others bent on polluting and extorting the public which, as we noted in the introduction (p. 15–18), carries some of the lingering legacies of the colonial gaze. Bringing into view the way the state-sponsored developmentalist discourse has repositioned *hijra*s as sexually, genitally, and hormonally *protibondhi* ("handicapped" or "disabled") people in need of rescue and social protection, *hijra* culture has been framed in this dominant discourse as oppressive communitarian baggage impeding the social empowerment and livelihood development of *hijra*s. Echoing various colonial policies, the flurry of activities adopted by the Bangladeshi state now seeks to eradicate *hijragiri*, the *hijra* occupations, and thereby *badhai* and *cholla* (collection of monies and foodstuffs from the marketplaces), which publicly mark them as *hijra*s.

The observations upon which this chapter is predicated were conducted as part of fieldwork that has taken place from 2000 up to the time of writing. In this extended period, I have been involved in various capacities with *hijra*s in the capital city of Dhaka and beyond in Bangladesh. At times I was invited to be an amanuensis registering names and gifts at special *hijra* festivals to which *hijra*s from various other houses from Bangladesh and India were invited, and at other times I was asked to be a bridge between donors interested in setting up community-based organizations and *hijra*s. On many occasions, I was also invited to be a photographer capturing special moments at ceremonies including *badhai* performances while at other times, I was simply asked by my *hijra* interlocutors to observe their performances at a safe distance and act as if I was not with the *hijra* troupe. There were however moments when the members of the households being visited by *hijra* troupes for *badhai* sought my intervention to convince *hijra*s to lower their demands or simply leave. This long immersion into the *hijra* universe in Dhaka and beyond enabled me to witness shifts in socio-cultural as well as NGO and state attitude towards *badhai*. For example, while households in urban middle-class Dhaka approached by *hijra*s for *badhai* would often call the local police to rescue them from the presence of *hijra*s, the police were known to mediate between the two parties, often by asking the complainants to pay the *hijra*s an amount lower than what the *hijra*s had demanded. In contrast, today police may apprehend *hijra* troupes on the ground of extortion and public nuisance in light of the recent policy of the Bangladeshi government forbidding these practices in the aftermath of their legal recognition. This chapter foregrounds these shifts, first by describing the ritual context in which such performances are embedded and then by turning to the way the discourses of empowerment and developmentalism have been mobilized to refashion *hijra*s into respectable and productive citizens. Central to this developmentalist initiative is an attempt to reframe *hijra*s as hindrances to their own empowerment by reaffirming the "real/fake" *hijra* dichotomies wherein the "fake ones" need to be uprooted for the "real *hijra*s" to be rescued. This chapter ends by indicating that the continued insistence on and participation in *badhai* performance by *hijra*s is a testament to how *hijra*s transform the societally approved state-sponsored interpellation of them as disabled into various affective world-making abilities.

Ritual Contexts

In December 2019, I accompanied a three-member *hijra* troupe to observe their *badhai* performance in a semi-urban working-class neighborhood in the old part of Dhaka, the historic city on the banks of the Buriganga river that was once the center of commercial activities. After thirty minutes of walking through various backstreets, we reached a multi-storeyed building next to a Muslim seminary. The *hijra*s already had information about the birth of a male child in that house based on previous knowledge of this family. The household with the newborn was on the second floor. Bonna *hijra* entered the flat as the gate was already open, while Shewly and Trisha remained outside seated on the staircase. Shewly had a *dhol* (a double-headed drum that *hijra*s deem sacrosanct) hung around their neck. After a while, Bonna came out with the child despite the family's refusal to hand the newborn to them. As soon as Bonna returned, Trisha stood up and began singing a popular Bangla song and clapping rhythmically while Shewly played the drum seated on the stairs. A man, seemingly in his mid-thirties, came along and started arguing with the *hijra* entourage about how they should come back another time since the father of the child was away, and that there was no-one in the house to pay them the 3000 taka (approx. $35) that the *hijra*s were demanding. He claimed that he was only the uncle of the child, and was not in a position to pay them. In the meantime, next-door neighbors came out to see the spectacle, piqued by the commotion that had ensued after Bonna got into a verbal fight with the newborn's uncle and the brief musical performance had come to a halt. By then the trio figured out that the man claiming to be the newborn's uncle was in fact the father of the newborn. Caught red-handed, the father started entreating them to come back another day as he would really like to pay but did not have any money left in the house. Bonna started hurling profanities at him for his earlier falsehood, while Trisha took him to task for having impregnated his wife in the first place and having fathered a child without being mindful of his dues to the *hijra*s. Haggling ensued between the *hijra* ensemble and the householder until the father gave in and went downstairs to fetch money from a local shop. Five minutes later, he returned with 2500 taka (approx. $29) and handed it to Bonna. Without further ado, Bonna, Shewly, and Trisha left the building, warning the man in the house that they would return to collect the remaining amount with interest another day.

Later on, on our way back to their *guru*'s house, Bonna told me that in case of refusal by the householders (the father of the child in this case) or any other senior member in the absence of the father, they would typically resort to serious bargaining with the household and highly sexualized insult (*chitti*) in a bid to coerce them into paying them their *badhai* gift. For example, Trisha had earlier mentioned to the newborn's father that had he married and fucked one of them, he would not have to pay such a fee since *hijras* cannot beget children. Shewly also insulted an old man who had shown up suddenly from downstairs to speak to the newborn's father, asking if he would like to marry one of them and enjoy his old age being pampered in a *hijra* house. Bonna explained to me that they chose to leave the household without much bargaining as the householder (father) was not wealthy enough and they had other houses to go to. More importantly, while *hijra* ensembles typically perform (singing, dancing, and playing the *dhol*) before making their demands, they refrained from putting up an elaborate performance at this specific household since they did not want their labor to be undervalued—they had been at this household previously but were denied any *badhai* gift.

That Bonna, Trisha, and Shewly resorted to hurling abuse at the householder is quite a common phenomenon. In some *badhai* situations that I have participated in, the *hijra* troupe put a curse on the household, invoking deities to punish them since they denied the *hijras* their rightful share. Most typical curses by *hijras* involve the trope of male children or yet-to-be-born male heirs becoming *hijras*. The cursing strategies and sexualized verbal insolence used by the *hijras* often zone in on male sexual prowess and masculine deficiency, instilling in the household a sense of fear that the newborn may also grow up to be like them, a possibility that the householders typically wish to thwart, and therefore bow down to *hijra* demands (Hossain 2021: 73). On one occasion during a *badhai* that I observed, one *hijra* undressed themself and sat naked in front of the household after they refused to give in to their demands. To avoid embarrassment, the householder rushed to the nearby shop to borrow money and paid the *hijra* group. Anthropologist Kira Hall (1997) contends that the use of verbal insults by *hijras* in their encounters with the mainstream population allows them to reclaim a space normally unavailable to them. *Hijras* participating in such sexualized insulting banter also challenge the dominant cartographies of gender and sexuality that are otherwise employed to marginalize them.

Bonna, Trisha, and Shewly are all *cela*s (also spelled *chela*) of Srabonti, a *hijra guru* who is not only a *sadrali* (those who conduct *hijragiri*, i.e. eke out a living by conducting *badhai* and *cholla*) but also a part-time dance teacher beyond the lineage. While *sadrali*s typically refrain from engaging in activities that are unrelated to *hijrapon* or *hijra* occupation, Srabonti continued to be a dance teacher for children in a dance academy from the onset of their initiation into the *hijra* universe. The very morning I arrived at their house in old Dhaka to accompany their *cela*s to observe their *badhai* activities, they[3] had returned from Kolkata where they had been to participate in *hijragiri* as well as one dance show with the children. Srabonti lived in their current rented house along with Shewly, Bonna, and Shriti. This abode serves as the *dera* where their other *cela*s and sometimes even their *guru* gather (see Pamment's chapter for an exposition on *dera*). Like Srabonti, Shewly, Bonna, and Trisha are all part-time dancers whom Srabonti has coached. Srabonti explained to me that for them, conducting the *hijra* occupation (*pesha pon*, or *hijragiri*) was paramount and it was their source of strength for the person that they became. Even though they had been a dance teacher in the same neighborhood, they maintained that this line of work never took precedence over their *hijra* vocation. This apparent incompatibility between being a dance teacher and being a *hijra* that Srabonti hinted at made sense to me when Shewly and Shriti later explained that although dancing and singing are part of their occupation, working as individual performers in various social functions is not part of their *hijra* occupation. Although Srabonti makes a distinction here between being a dance teacher and a *sadrali hijra*, the boundary between these two lines of work is often fluid as the training/skills cultivated elsewhere potentially feed *badhai* and vice versa. In addition to being part-time dancers, Shewly, Shriti, Bonna, and Trisha also occasionally do sex work. While they all perform *badhai* and *cholla* within a *birit*, the ritual jurisdiction within which a *hijra* group is allowed to operate as *hijra*s, work as a dance teacher, an individual performer, and/ or as a sex worker is not tied to similar territorial boundaries.

Like Srabonti's *cela*s, *hijra* groups in Dhaka undertake *badhai* work at least twice a week, while on the rest of the days they conduct *cholla* depending on the number and size of bazaars a *birit* boasts. *Badhai* performance in Bangladesh typically takes place among families of the working-class on the occasions of births. Unlike in India and Pakistan, *badhai* rarely takes place during marriage celebrations in contemporary Bangladesh. While roaming around within the *birit*, *hijra* groups are often on the lookout for signs that there may be a household with a pregnant woman or that a child has been born. The sighting of a "*falia*," the *hijra* word for small patches of cloth used to wrap a newborn, often hung on a clothesline outside the house or in the veranda to dry, is a clear indication for prospective *badhai* performance. Once spotted, *hijra*s then visit the household to demand *badhai*. Nevertheless, Trisha and Bonna drew my attention to the fact that in urban middle- and upper-class families and households to which they are generally denied access (I say more about this class politics later in this chapter) clothes are washed in the washing machines and then hung in the drawing room to dry, making it difficult for *hijra*s to discern the arrival of a newborn.

The *hijra* ensemble both for *badhai* and *cholla* typically consists of three members. A *badhai* ensemble carries a *dhol* and its members must have the skills to dance and sing; however, such a combination is not necessary for *cholla* since singing and dancing are not part of it, and nor, therefore, are *dhol*s carried. A *cholla* troupe typically trawls through the bazaar and picks up fruits, vegetables, and cash mainly from the vendors. While erotic banter and fondling are part of the standard interactional repertoire of *hijra*s when engaging the vendors (Hossain 2021: 76–7), the scope for bargaining is limited as a roving *hijra* group has to cover quite a lot of ground. In the case of *badhai*, however, one member forces their way into the house to take the child before returning with them into the courtyard, while another member starts to sing and dance to the sound of the drum, which is played by a third member of the entourage. After the dance with the newborn, the dance-performing *hijra* goes back inside the house to bring some mustard oil with which they then anoint the child's head, all the while chanting out mantras intended to wish the child and the family good health and longevity at a very high speed. *Hijra*s also adjust the mantra accordingly depending on the religious background of the household. While in a Muslim household, mantras invoked revolve around entreating Allah to bless the child and its family, mantras recited in a Hindu household call upon Hindu deities. Typically, *hijra*s recite the mantras so fast that their syllables become indecipherable for the spectators. However, since many working-class households are not able to afford mustard oil these days, *hijra*s are often forced to perform the blessing without it.

In certain commercial areas in urban Dhaka where a *birit* may consist mostly of offices and markets and no households, *cholla* becomes the dominant form of *hijra* occupation. For *badhai*, *hijra*s make a rapid assessment of the economic status of the household based on the occupation of the householder as well as the various goods and furniture in the household. The gifts demanded, therefore, vary according to the socio-economic position of the household being visited, whereas the scope for making huge financial demands is limited during *cholla*. Nevertheless, twice in the year on the special occasions of two Muslim Eid festivals, *hijra*s make greater demands on the vendors and stallholders. Although there is the generic rule to perform *cholla* thrice and *badhai* twice a week as indicated earlier, it varies in practice depending on how resource-poor or wealthy one's *birit* is.

Like the *khwaja sira*s in Pakistan that Pamment's chapter elucidates, the kind of performance that *badhai* practitioners in Dhaka present hinges very much on the social background of the household. For example, if the visited household is Hindu, then the *hijra* ensemble sing songs that are recognizably

Hindu—while in the case of a Muslim household, the references within the same songs can change to those of Islam. A song I had seen several *hijra* troupes perform during *badhai* went as follows:[4]

> O sister is it a boy or a girl?
> Aunties of the boy and the girl have all been informed
> We are here to dance with drums
> In an unknown country, nature has created a hijra
> Now the hijras have come with drum and harmonium to
>   dance
> O sister is it a boy or a girl?

What is interesting about the above lyrics is that translation of some of the words and expressions into Bangla can be both Hindu and Muslim-identified. An example here is the word "nature" in the fourth line of the song, which *hijra*s can replace with either *Allah* or *Vagoban* (Muslim and Hindu marked names respectively) depending on the socio-religious background of the household. In a similar vein, words like "sister" and "aunties" can also be translated into various versions of Bangla that may be seen culturally as either Hindu or Muslim. The kind of songs and lyrics *hijra*s use also depends on the gender of the newborn. For example, if the newborn is male, *hijra* groups will often sing a song that likens the newborn to a full moon and that such a gift is reminiscent of the blessings of prophet Muhammad; if the newborn is female, the theme of a popular song sung by *hijra*s concerns how the female child would not have to pay rent if she could become a landlady (through marriage) and how it would be impossible for her to keep hold of her youthfulness.

A common theme that *badhai*-performing *hijra* troupes in Dhaka often asserted to me was that *hijra*s in India could demand and earn considerably more during *badhai* celebrations than in Bangladesh, as *hijra*s enjoyed greater respect among the Indian populace. *Hijra*s in Bangladesh often argue that the greater social respect that *hijra*s enjoy in India is due to the fact that the *hijra* occupation originally stems from Hinduism and that Hindus regard *hijra*s as god-like figures. This is not to suggest, however, that *hijra*s do not identify with Islam. In fact as I argued elsewhere (Hossain 2012), there is no homogenous cultural or religious identification for Bangladeshi *hijra*s, who, despite being born Muslims, worship Hindu-marked goddesses, and yet do not see themselves as Hindu. Rather they glean creatively from both Muslim and Hindu tradition to craft their cosmology just like their Indian counterparts (see Reddy 2005 for more on this).[5] For example, in one corner of Srabonti's *dera* was an altar upon which were two *dhol*s. Next to these *dhol*s was a framed poster of a *hijra* goddess perched on a rooster (known as both Bahuchara Mata and Bedraj Mata in India and as Maya Ji and Tara Moni in Bangladeshi *hijra* cosmogony, Hossain 2021: 112–15) and a large picture of a naked Muslim saint, believed to be spiritually linked with Khaja Moinuddin Chisti, that *hijra*s as well as many Sufi-oriented Muslims in Bangladesh venerate. Before going out to perform *hijragiri*, Srabonti and their *cela*s would pay respect not only to the *dhol*s but also to Maya Ji, Tara Moni, and the Muslim saints. Showing respect for as well as invoking these saints and goddesses are what sets apart the *hijra* occupation from other activities, Srabonti elaborated.

As explained in the discussion on the supra-national *hijrascape* in the introduction of this book (p. 29–32), *hijra* subjectivities in Bangladesh, just as in India and Pakistan, are woven through various symbolic and material comings and goings (Hossain 2018; Hossain and Nanda 2020). Several of my *hijra* interlocutors have not only visited various Indian *hijra* houses, especially those in West Bengal and Delhi, but also have worked in India as part of various *hijra* lineages before returning to Bangladesh. Srabonti, for example, is the *cela* of Pushpo Haji, a renowned *hijra guru* in Bangladesh who is alleged to have built a house on the outskirts of Dhaka with earnings obtained during their seven-year stint as a *hijra* in Delhi. I have also noticed several Indian *hijra*s visiting *hijra* houses in Bangladesh for ritual and social purposes. While the flows of people, goods, and ideas within the wider network of material and symbolic relations inform the *hijra* subject position across South Asia, the frequent referencing of India by my interlocutors as the primordial and ideal location where *hijra*s are celebrated can be seen as an example of an elsewhere (see Roy and Pamment's discussion of elsewhere in their respective chapters) that functions both as a sign of their abjected status in Bangladesh today and as a space for imagining and reformulating a futurity in the face of a dwindling clientele (more on this in the next section).

Jomuna, a venerable *hijra guru* who passed away a few years ago, once explained to me that whether a household would pay the requested *badhai* or not depends on the way an ensemble performed on the spot. Nostalgic about how *jodgman*[6] (the non-*hijra* populace at large) in the British and Pakistan era

FIGURE 5 *Jomuna* guru *performing a Hindi song while playing the* dhol, *showing their artistic skills to inspire their* celas *in their* dera *in Dhaka, 2012 (Photo: Adnan Hossain).*

would shower them with gifts and monies, they bemoaned the lack of skills and the abilities of their *nati* (grand) and *puti* (great-grand) *cela*s in postcolonial Bangladesh to improvise, sing songs, and dance in keeping with the background and sensibilities of the households being visited. They went on to describe to me *kula nachano*—literally, *kula* dance—a standard item of *badhai* practice now on the decline. A *kula* is a basket made of bamboo used to winnow rice or grain from the chaff. Households are expected to fill a *kula* with rice, potatoes, vegetables, garlic, and onions and hand it over to the visiting *hijra* ensemble. A *hijra* performs a whirling dance with the kula full of items received from the household without a single grain being dropped from the basket. Once the performance is over, a *hijra* places the items from the *kula* into a red sack (*oli*) and returns the *kula* along with some rice. *Hijra*s believe that a small portion of the total foodstuffs received must be handed back immediately to the household so that the "good fortune" of the household is not compromised (Hossain 2021: 68). While Jomuna berated their *cela*s because of their inability to perform and live up to this artistic standard and aesthetics, their *cela*s related to me a different story; namely, that the gradual disappearance of the *kula* dance as part of the *badhai* repertoire was in fact due to the congested urban housing in Dhaka and lack of courtyards—making it almost impossible for the *badhai* ensembles to sing and dance, let alone undertake the *kula* dance. Moreover, they informed me that most households in urban areas no longer use *kula*.

This trope of decline in relation to *hijragiri*, and especially *badhai*, figured most prominently each time a *hijra* ensemble seeking to perform *badhai* encountered hostility from the public. Such opposition to *hijra* presence is most pronounced in urban middle-class spaces, to which *hijra*s are generally denied access. Not only are these middle- and upper-middle-class households often gated, they are also the ones with the most antagonistic attitude towards the *hijra*s and their performance practices that have become a new target of state and societal vilification, as explained in the next section.

Legal Recognition and Social Development

In a flyer titled "The Livelihood Development Program of *Hijra* (Transgender) Community" published in 2018 by the Ministry of Social Welfare, *hijra*s are defined as "congenitally sexually handicapped people who, because of either genetic or physical conditions, cannot be classified as either male or female. Chromosomal anomalies are the main cause for the birth of such sexually defective people."[7] Furthermore, the flyer provides a description of *hijra* culture (including *badhai*) in South Asia as a way to contextualize government activities. Significantly, the flyer describes *badhai* as a "collection of gifts by use of mild force," and "payment/gifts received in exchange for blessings" as traditional *hijra* activity. These activities undertaken by the government are intended to enhance the competence and skills of the *hijra* population so that they can be involved in various mainstream income-generating activities instead of resorting to *badhai* and *cholla*. Examples include special training programs offered by the government in collaboration with NGOs in the following fields: paramedicine, hairdressing, beautification, driving, mobile phone repair, TV, freezer and air conditioning repairs, automobile industry, security guard, Ansar and VDP (a paramilitary auxiliary force), nursing, portering, agriculture, fishery and livestock management, computing, sewing and cutting in the garments and textile sector, boutique work, and handicrafts.

The government of Bangladesh rolled out a broad program in the fiscal year 2012–13 to be implemented by the Ministry of Social Welfare for the development of the livelihood of the *hijra* populace. Significantly, state allocation for the various activities intended to mainstream the *hijra* population has progressively increased since the *hijra*s' legal recognition in 2013. For example, while during the 2012–13 fiscal year such allocations were part of a pilot project of the Ministry of Social Welfare, activities to mainstream them became part of the regular social safety net programs of the Ministry of Social Welfare by the fiscal year 2015–16 (interview with the Ministry of Social Welfare 2019). *Hijra*s also appear as a socially excluded people in the National Social Security Strategy (NSSS) of Bangladesh, a national strategy paper approved by the cabinet on June 1, 2015 (General Economics Division Planning Commission Government of the People's Republic of Bangladesh, 2015: 23, 58, 64, 68).[8] The main vision of the government is to build social safety measures for all deserving citizens, particularly the poor and vulnerable, to make the country free from hunger and poverty.

The incorporation of *hijra*s within discourses and policies of developmentalist intervention engenders mechanisms for *hijra*s to become a new target of control in which traditional *hijra* ways and culture are seen as hindering their social development (see also Puri 2010). While in the era before the legal recognition of *hijra*s in 2013, NGOs and government bodies engaged *hijra*s as an at-risk social group in the context of STD and HIV prevention work, the view of both NGOs and various bodies of the government in the post-recognition phase has been through the lens of social development. Importantly, a new discourse of disability had to be mobilized and institutionalized at the official level in order for *hijra*s to emerge as an intelligible subject of development. Elsewhere I elaborate on the cultural politics and paradox of the legal recognition of *hijra*s (Hossain 2017); here I want to focus mainly on the way *hijra*s have been catapulted into a "new kind of visibility" (Escobar 1995) as a socially excluded people after their legal recognition as a distinct sex/gender.

Refiguring *hijra*s as a new subject of development here corresponds to the current Bangladesh government's (in power since January 2009) vision of Bangladesh as a middle-income country, free from poverty and with healthy and equitable growth, secure health and education, entrenched democracy, and the capacity to meet the challenges of climate change. In her special message for the publication of the

NSSS of Bangladesh in July 2015, Sheikh Hasina, the current head of the state, writes:

> As Bangladesh has already been declared as a lower middle-income country, we are fully committed to improving our status to upper middle-income country well before the targeted 2021. The National Social Security Strategy is central to our Vision 2021 and will play a vital role in ensuring growth with equity as we move towards this target.
>
> (ii–iii)

Although social development has been part of Bangladesh's national strategy from the time of its birth in 1971, the present social development paradigm adopted by the government of Bangladesh needs to be seen in the context of the current regime's intention to employ social development as a tool to make up for its democratic deficit. From this perspective, the targeting of *hijra*s as a socially excluded group can be seen as tokenism, since it is part of a strategy to target various socially excluded and minority communities to "build Bangladesh into a resilient, productive, innovative, and prosperous nation with a caring society consisting of healthy, happy, and well-educated people" (General Economics Division Planning Commission Government of the People's Republic of Bangladesh, 2010: 1).

This framework of social development views *hijragiri* as a serious obstacle to *hijra*s' social empowerment and livelihood development. As previously argued, activities such as *badhai* and *cholla* are conceived as forms of begging and extortion devoid of religious and ritual meaning. Here, the intention of the state to curtail *hijragiri* corresponds to their plans to eradicate begging from the streets of major cities, including the capital city of Dhaka. In October 2016, the government vowed to rehabilitate 21,889 beggars in Khulna by December of the following year. A rehabilitation centre, with training and healthcare facilities, was set up on a 15-acre plot of land, and 20,282 beggars were indeed rehabilitated there by May 2017 (Saadat 2018), while beggars were paid to be off the streets in Chittagong, a southeastern city in Bangladesh, during the Cricket World Cup in 2011 (Ahmed 2011). In 2010, the government considered banning begging and making it a punishable offence—but backtracked after the move was considered a human rights violation (Devnath 2019). Signs against begging have popped up all over the city. The government has also declared certain areas of the capital, such as VIP roads, military garrisons, diplomatic zones, and residential areas like Banani, Gulshan, Baridhara, Dhanmondi, and Ramna to be free from beggars, while anti-begging drives are periodically conducted by the police in conjunction with the Department of Social Services, a wing of the Ministry of Social Welfare entrusted with the task of eradicating begging (Debnath 2017). Although such anti-begging activities do not target *hijra*s directly, these actions have repercussions for *hijra*s' access to certain areas, which in turn restricts their practice of *cholla* and *badhai*.

Consistent with the spirit of state-sponsored social development aimed at refashioning *hijra*s into respectable regular citizens, a host of NGOs and private initiatives have sprung up in the aftermath of their legal recognition. A notable initiative is the setting up of a foundation in 2012 called "*Hizra Kallyan* Foundation" (literally, Foundation for *Hijra* Welfare) by Abida Sultana Meetu, a female leader affiliated with the ruling Bangladesh Awami League party. In an interview in December 2019, Meetu explained to me the vision of the foundation and its activities. According to her,

> Begging needs to stop. There is no state sanctioned policy to support badhai or cholla. These are extortions and ought to be eradicated. If necessary, police need to be mobilized to prevent the roaming hijra groups from demanding alms from the people. Hijras are rarely sighted in this area as begging as the police have taken strict measures including beating the loitering hijras up.

She further stated that "special training programs are necessary to help hijras change their behavior so that they do not misbehave with the public and stop demanding alms and badhai. We also need to track the assets owned by the hijra gurus and the source of their income." Mahi, a *hijra guru* in Motijhil also present during this interview, later related to me that those who accuse the *hijra gurus* of being owners of unscrupulously obtained wealth should understand that *hijras* have been able to accumulate wealth and assets not only through their hard work of *badhai* and *cholla* but also through inheritance from their *gurus* who in turn inherited from their *gurus*. Echoing many others, Mahi contended that the state initiatives to rehabilitate and mainstream *hijras* are not sustainable, as very few *hijras* have ever been successful in working in a mainstream occupation without being bullied and stigmatized in spite of whatever training might have been given.

To prevent *hijras* from collecting alms, the foundation in question sought help from the police. Meetu took out a letter from a drawer and showed it to me during our meeting in Dhaka. With her permission, I took a screenshot of the letter. Excerpts from the letter the foundation prepared and submitted to the police in 2017 are as follows in translation:

I, Abida Sultana Meetu, the founder of Hizra Kallyan Foundation, want to draw your attention to the fact that in November 2013, Sheikh Hasina, the prime minister of Bangladesh legally recognized the hijras as a third gender [...] At present some male persons beg in public impersonating hijras and engage in snatching and hijacking. These people are also involved in the collection of money from shops and marketplaces as well as dancing for the newborn in households. However, there is no legal basis for such activities. The general public are deeply harassed and dissatisfied because of these activities. Consequently, the reputation of my foundation is also being tainted. I therefore request you to kindly instruct all the police stations to take action so that such activities come to an end.

The recent developmentalist interventions have had a direct impact on the status of *badhai* and *cholla* work. Srabonti asserted, "These days when we go out to demand badhai or cholla, the public just shoo us away on the grounds that the government has recognized us and that we are now all provided for but that is all untrue"; while Trisha said, "The public mistakes the legal recognition as a state-sanctioned guarantee that we are all taken care of while in fact these initiatives have in many ways undermined our position and occupation." Interestingly, although state and civil society-supported programs today are intended to eliminate the *hijra* occupation as part of the developmentalist vision of a new Bangladesh, the recent economic boom and the surge of conspicuous consumption have paradoxically engendered new incentives for the *hijra* groups to demand *badhai* and *cholla*.

For example, collection of money at traffic lights was not a popular practice among *hijra*s in urban areas until recently. Nor was the traffic intersection seen as part of the *birit*. Today various *hijra* groups not only demand *cholla* from the bazaar but also at traffic lights and major intersections in urban Dhaka. My *hijra* interlocutors argue that since *hijra*s are not allowed to visit the middle-class houses and conduct *badhai* or perform on any other auspicious occasions, traffic lights and intersections are the only sites where they can place their demand on the middle- and upper-classes. Mahi further teased it out for me one evening.

> People today are scared of us. They do not even allow us to get past the main gate, let alone enter their houses and take the children in our laps. They think we will run away with the newborn and then demand a ransom. They think we are beggars and thieves. Badhai income is on the wane. It is with cholla money that we are sustaining hijragiri but these hijras demanding at traffic lights are a disputed territory. These are not part of our hijra occupation and any group is entitled to traffic interactions, so disputes often break out.

Disputes among the *hijra* groups in Dhaka and beyond about access to areas for collection of money and contestation over authentic *hijra* status have figured prominently in the wake of this recent social developmentalist discourse. As previously explained, *hijra*s operate within ritually marked jurisdictions and collect *cholla* and *badhai* within those designated territories. Conducting *badhai* and/or *cholla* beyond one's jurisdiction, known as *birit bakhor* (literally, stealing from one's area), is considered a serious crime. *Birit bakhor* often leads to disputes and physical fighting among *hijra* groups, for which special dispute resolution sessions may also be held. Genital status—whether one is emasculated or not—often emerges as the most significant trope in such disputes and "thieving" *hijra*s are often beaten up and shamed in public by *hijra* groups claiming to have rightful ownership of the territory (Hossain 2012). A popular shaming technique in such cases is to forcibly undress the thieving *hijra*s (especially if they are non-emasculated) before the ordinary people. Videos of *hijra* groups catching "fake *hijra*s" red-handed and shaming them in public are often circulated via various digital platforms across the South Asian transregional *hijrascape*. Such videos bring into view not only the lineage-sanctioned protocols of *hijragiri* but also the various hierarchical lines along which *hijra* communities are configured (I elaborate on this later in this chapter).

Such intra-community feuds can be explained with respect to a group's dependence on control of resources within a given jurisdiction and the declining base of social patrons willing to support the *hijra* occupation. Noteworthy here is the fact that monies collected from sex work or any other engagement, for example, individual performances as a dancer, as noted previously, or even NGO-related work that many *sadrali hijra*s today are involved in, are not handed back to the *guru*s, nor are they used for the purpose of *hijragiri*.[9] *Sadrali hijra*s not only distinguish themselves from *hijra*s that are sex workers (*dhurrani*) but also berate those engaged in sex work in the worst possible terms—even though the line between these two groups is often blurred in practice (Hossain 2021). *Sadrali hijra*s contend that association with prostitution works to compromise their ritual power by undermining their carefully guarded reputation of being asexual and above desire. While it is through a mobilization of a discourse of asexuality and them being above and beyond desire that *hijra*s in Dhaka legitimize their demand for both *badhai* and *cholla* collections in public (see also Nanda 1999 for a similar observation), such claims are often contradicted by examples of *hijra badhai* performances that are often highly sexualized, a paradox that I enlarge upon elsewhere (Hossain 2021).

The recent proliferation of *hijra*s demanding and collecting monies at traffic signals has led to frequent reporting in the print and television media on the public's encounter with *hijra*s. A news item published in an English-language daily called *Daily Sun* on August 16, 2018 is titled "Nuisance in public places by *hijra*s sharply rising." Excerpts from this news item read as follows:

> Monty Paul, a private job holder, was hanging out with her boyfriend on the bank of Dhanmondi Lake one fine evening last month. Suddenly, three hijras appeared before them clapping hands in a scary manner and sought Tk 200 from them. Nervous, Monty quickly offered them Tk 50 which only made the trio furious and they started hurling abuses at them. "Later, I gave the hijras Tk 100 but they again refused to accept it. Even, one of them said if you don't pay us Tk 200 we would curse you so that you can't get married and be happy. Finally, we gave them Tk 200 to get rid of the nuisance," Monty said, narrating her horrific experience.
>
> Abdul Mukith, a journalist, was welcoming guests who came to his Merul Badda residence three months back as he arranged a programme to name his newborn girl. The joyous mood of the house changed right away as a group of hijras stormed into it seeking Tk 5,000, marking the birth of his baby girl. At one stage, the *hijra*s tried to forcefully take

the baby in their laps to perform a dance. As the relatives shut the door of the room where the child was sleeping, the rowdy *hijra*s started knocking on it and shouting, creating a complete nuisance. Out of fear and embarrassment, Mukith said, he gave the *hijra*s Tk 4,000 to get relief of [sic] the nuisance.

The experience of Moinuddin Khokan, a government employee, was more disgusting and horrifying. Like other days, Moin said, he was going to his office at the Secretariat by a [sic] rickshaw barely two months back. "I got stuck in a traffic jam at Kakrail crossing and a hijra came forward seeking money from me. As I refused to pay, the angry hijra suddenly touched my sensitive organ and kept pressing my testicles hard. I had to give Tk 20 to save myself."

[...] These are only a few of the incidents of growing nuisance by hijras the city dwellers experience every day in the capital [...] The hijras also collect money from shops and business establishments every week. Visiting city's Kakrail, Gulshan, Motijheel, Mohalkhai, Gulshan, Banani, Farmgate, Dhanmondi, Agargaon, Mirpur, Bijoy Sarani and Mohammadpur areas, it was found that the hijras were collecting money from the commuters. Females who ride rickshaws, CNGs or buses without any male accompanying them are their prime target to extort money. As the hijra nuisance has turned unbearable, two female MPs raised the issue in Parliament on June 5, seeking a remedy. Quazi Rosy MP (reserved seat-41) narrated her bad experience saying some hijras threatened to shoot her as she refused to pay them money when they stormed into her Dhanmondi residence. Later, Commerce Minister Tofail Ahmed told Parliament that the government will take effective steps to prevent hijras from creating trouble in public places and houses to realise [sic] money by force.

This excerpt is representative of myriad reports and news items that appear regarding the public's encounters with *hijra*s in Dhaka. The demonization of *hijra*s in the above news item is not only reminiscent of the late nineteenth-century British colonial and Indian middle-class moral panic regarding *hijra*s (Hinchy 2019) but also of the abject othering in the politics of neoliberal progress to which *hijra*s are subject in recent times, as explicated in the introduction to this book (p. 22–26). More importantly, the dominant Bangladeshi social imagination posits the *hijra*s as foul-smelling, dirty, violent, and shameless people, and it is through the lens of their lower-class status, together with its associated images of filth, foul smell, cheap and gaudy makeup, and aggressiveness, that *hijra*s are discursively demonized in middle-class imaginary (Hossain 2017; 2021). Such demonization also directly contributes to their material and social deprivation—a fact evident in how *hijra*s in Dhaka often struggle to rent a house or room even in the most squalid of neighborhoods (Hossain and Esthappan 2021).

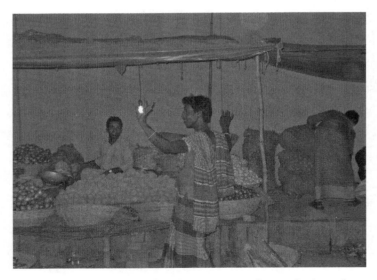

FIGURE 6 *Doyeli* hijra *entertaining a vendor with their dance moves during* cholla *collection in a bazaar in Dhaka, 2018 (Photo: Adnan Hossain).*

While the society at large views *badhai/cholla* with suspicion and dismisses these activities as extortion and begging, *hijras* continue to insist on these practices being sacred and imbued with religious significance. Based on their fieldwork in India, Saria (2019) contends that it is reductive to read the *hijra* practice of *cholla* merely through the lens of secular forms of begging, as the training offered by *hijra gurus* to young *hijras* recasts the exchange of money from begging to *cholla*, and in so doing undoes the stigma attached to begging. Saria further notes that the practice of demanding *cholla* is a complex religious economic exchange that requires "calibration of coercion, placation, humor, and sartorial presentation," traits that clearly set *cholla* apart from general forms of begging regularly seen in public space across South Asia. In a similar vein, as I explicate elsewhere (2021, p. 76–77), the *hijra* practice of trawling through the marketplaces is an agentic act that works to engender a carnivalesque atmosphere in the bazaar. The erotic innuendoes and sexualized banter that the roving *hijra* groups direct towards the vendors and the householders while demanding *cholla* and *badhai* animates and lightens the mood of the clientele, features that clearly mark *cholla* and *badhai* as distinct forms of exchange and gifting relation premised on a complex moral economy not reducible to regular forms of begging.

Nevertheless, the recent set of developmentalist initiatives undertaken in the wake of their legal recognition has deemed *hijragiri* as antithetical to the logics of neoliberal progress and citizenship, reaffirming "real/fake" *hijra* dichotomies, to which the next section turns.

Hijragiri as a New Target of Control

Although tropes of ambiguity, subterfuge, and fakery figure routinely in the context of inter/intra-community bickering and dispute over access to and control of resources and territorial boundaries (Hossain 2012; Reddy 2005), the social development model to mainstream the *hijra*s has engendered a new impetus to distinguish the "real" *hijra*s from the "fake" ones (Pamment forthcoming b). Here, the immediate background to the recent state interest in screening and identifying real *hijra*s stems from the way a project initiated by the government in the aftermath of the legal recognition of the *hijra*s to recruit fourteen of them as low-ranking clerks or peons was terminated after a medical screening revealed that all the applicants were male except one who had a penis and scrotum.[10] The results of the medical examination established for the government and the wider society that these were male-bodied people impersonating *hijra*s in a bid to access resources that are actually meant for the real *hijra*s (Hossain 2017).

Against this backdrop, the Ministry of Social Welfare, in conjunction with the Ministry of Health and Family Planning, have taken initiatives to institutionalize screening processes at various state-funded establishments so that only real *hijra*s are able to benefit from and access various government and NGO-supported social programs. The field level units of the Ministry of Health perform the task of screening and identifying *hijra*s at various local levels. While it is still not clear how such screening takes place in these governmental establishments and whether there is a uniform screening protocol (since there are differing accounts from *hijra*s that have been subjected to this procedure), several *hijra* groups have already objected to such screening procedures via various social and activist platforms. Nevertheless, the Ministry of Social Welfare continues to hold on to and emphasize the importance of medical screening as a necessary step towards establishing the real number of *hijra*s in Bangladesh. Once a person undergoes the screening and is identified as a *hijra*, they are then issued a certificate authenticating their *hijra* status. The holders of such certificates are then able to participate in the various state-initiated training programs.[11]

The impetus for the state-supported policy initiatives to perform gender testing and screening derives from the government's understanding and definition of *hijra*s as people born with missing or ambiguous genitals, as previously explained. While realness or authentic *hijra* status is often associated with one's bodily state of being emasculated in the Indian context (Nanda 1999; Reddy 2005), such a status is deemed in the Bangladeshi context as inauthentic and fake (Hossain 2017; 2012). This debate over fake versus real *hijra*s in the national parliament of Bangladesh in 2018 reignited a public and media interest in the question about who is and is not a real *hijra* and that fake *hijra*s abound in Bangladeshi society that need to be eliminated in order for the real *hijra*s to be salvaged. More importantly, the concept of fake *hijra*, activated in the aftermath of legal recognition of *hijra*s and the subsequent embrace of the social development model, works to perpetuate what Pamment (forthcoming b) in the Pakistani context describes as "violent hierarchies of legitimacy both within public space and within internally diverse *hijra* communities."

One trope that emerged especially among the NGO, human rights, and development discourse in this regard posits that those who demand money at traffic lights are not real *hijra*s, and that furthermore, *they* are the ones mugging and stealing while real *hijra*s are given the blame. In a recent edited publication in Bangla on *hijra*s, a group of well-known public intellectuals and development practitioners in Bangladesh have made similar arguments about *hijra*s demanding money at traffic lights being fake. An excerpt from that edited collection is in translation below:

Collection of money from the public has become a fraudulent business. Because of chronic unemployment, many normal males are becoming *hijra*s artificially and they extort money from the people. Removing one's genitals and becoming an artificial *hijra* is a common practice in Bangladesh and in India. Typically, uneducated and unemployed males as well as effeminate males often fall prey to such practice. Sometimes, homosexually inclined young men can also be a victim of this practice. There are plenty of people who

were victimized. There are a few hospitals in Bangladesh
that create artificial *hijra*s. Nowadays these artificial *hijra*s
engage in extortion, looting, killing and drug trading.

(Ferdous et al. 2019: 136)

The above passage, redolent of the state-sanctioned discourse
within the so-called social development model keen on tackling
exclusion of real *hijra*s, actually reinforces and perpetuates
intra/inter-community conflicts and divisions and ends up
targeting and hurting those on the street and engaged in *hijragiri*,
including *badhai* and *cholla*. It also serves as an example of a
socio-economic logic mobilized within the development policy
to not only rationalize mainstreaming activities for *hijra*s but
also specifically target *badhai* and *cholla* as regressive practices
that need to be eradicated for *hijra*s to become respectable
neoliberal citizens (see also Roy 2016 and Pamment 2019b for
more on such respectable neoliberal citizenship in the Indian
and Pakistani contexts respectively).

This new process of gender screening and certification
brings genitals to the forefront in determining and assigning
one's status as a *hijra*—to the detriment of performance
and various actions and doings through which *hijraness* is
forged and performed within inter/intra-community contexts
(Hossain 2021). The disparagement of the *hijra* practices is
further evident in the emergence of a new trope among NGOs,
development and rights practitioners that positions *hijragiri* as
well as the adoption of a *hijra* subject position as a mere culture
rather than a gender, rendering the *hijra* subject position and
its associated rituals as forms of regressive communitarian
baggage that ought to be discouraged and eventually eliminated.
Here the state-initiated programs mentioned earlier are seen as
pathways for *hijra*s to come out of this backward culture and
to be involved in the productive economy. The accent on the
need to involve *hijra*s in the productive economy derives also
from the idea that *hijrapon*, or the *hijra* occupation, entails
no specific skill sets. Hridoy, a transgender-identified NGO
employee once remarked, "Badhai and cholla should be the
last resorts of hijras. If they can find employment, they would

not want to undertake those activities. As long as they do not gain the skills, they will continue to remain on the margin as beggars." Grudgingly pointing out the way they were denied their rightful share while being a part of *hijra* occupation in the past, Hridoy censured the hierarchical configuration of the *hijra* organization as tyrannical and enslaving (see also the discussion in Pamment's chapter on "enslaving structures" in the context of *dera* versus NGOs). While in former times, the mainstream society viewed the practitioners of *badhai* to be legitimate claimants to a *hijra* status, *badhai* in contemporary Bangladesh has come to emblematize both backwardness and fakeness. The idea here is that those with no skills are the ones that undertake *hijragiri* and they do so only because they are likely to fail the gender screening test to be eligible for social development pathways and become "respectable" citizens. In this framework, backwardness and fakeness co-constitute each other and only those that adopt the assimilationist model of respectable citizenship as defined by the state are seen as real *hijra*s.

While the social and cultural legitimacy for *badhai* and *cholla* derives from socio-religious belief in *hijra* sacred power, such a belief among the general populace has fallen into disuse and in its place has emerged developmentalism as the new social optic, which works to devalorize the *hijra* occupation. Bringing into view the way the *hijra* practices of *badhai* and *cholla* are on the decline in contemporary Bangladesh is not to suggest a teleological narrative in which a gilded past with its total acceptance and tolerance of *hijragiri* is now being supplanted by a present that is hostile towards and dismissive of *hijra*s and their occupational activities. Even though my *hijra* interlocutors often crafted a narrative of gradual decline of social respect towards them, and in which neighboring countries, especially India, were more approving of *hijra* practices, careful historical reading indicates that *hijra* has always been a site of struggle with society at large harboring ambivalent attitudes towards *hijra*s and their rituals and practices. It is therefore important not to lose sight of the fact that the recent state-sponsored social rescue model that bifurcates *hijra*s into real versus fake is an old tactic employed by both colonial and postcolonial states to eradicate *hijra*s at various points in South Asian history (Hinchy 2019; Pamment forthcoming b).

Badhai as Ability

Even though the socio-religious legitimacy for *badhai* and *cholla* is increasingly undermined in the face of new developmentalism and neoliberal citizenship rights, *hijra*s in Dhaka continue to insist on *badhai* and *cholla* as the ultimate occupation sanctioned by the divine. Mahi, involved in both *hijragiri* and NGO work, once remarked, "Badhai has a history of at least 500 years. It is our occupation. It is our livelihood. The government should enact regulations to protect our rights to conduct badhai." For many *hijra*s, *badhai* functions as a site through which they can express themselves, even if such expressions of skills and talent are not necessarily valorized by the clientele. When asked about why they practice *badhai* in a climate where such opportunities and spaces for the performances are under attack, Trisha and Srabonti contended, "We enjoy performing. There are particular pleasures associated with badhai and cholla. Becoming a hijra entails attainment of various kinds of skills. It is a way to express oneself. Material gain is transient but being part of this occupation is a source of strength." While *hijragiri*, including *badhai* and *cholla*, may be at the receiving end of state and social vilification in contemporary Bangladesh, the pleasures, performances, and history of *badhai* labor that the comments from Trisha, Mahi, and Srabonti point towards offer various affective world-making possibilities and pathways derived from and extending the South Asian transregional *hijrascape*.

2

Shifting Orientations: *Vadhai* in Pakistan

Claire Pamment

Openings

Oh Allah, protect us! Why is this door closed on downtrodden people like us? Allah has blessed you with happiness. What about us? When we were born, the doors of our houses were closed on us. Now why are you shutting doors on us? May Allah give you more if you give us something too! Since the time of our ancestors we have been coming to your door!

Naghma Gogi (August 2019)

Naghma Gogi, one of my close collaborators in the devised theater project *Teesri Dhun* (*The Third Tune*; Pamment et al. 2015; 2021), and recently celebrated as a transgender singer by Coke Studio, recounts an entry she would perform when confronted by reluctant patrons on rounds of *vadhai* (*badhai*)[1] in her youth. By reminding the householders of their previous relationships with the *khwaja sira* lineage, heralding their status as benevolent protectors of the downtrodden, and summoning Allah's blessings, Naghma begins to pry open the shut door. This chapter builds on efforts in this book to complicate the dominant neocolonial imaging of *badhai* as an act of extortion within narrow registers of shame and embarrassment, by emphasizing the weaving of affect and relationalities in Pakistani performance contexts. In the shifting entanglements around gender, class, religion, sexuality, kinship, and nation, I foreground the many affective possibilities of *vadhai* within and beyond Punjabi *ilaka* neighborhoods as performers navigate doors that may be closed to them, and/or already open through relationalities woven in performances across *khwaja sira* lineages.

The chapter elaborates *vadhai* in *ilaka* contexts as well as in national forums to engage *vadhai*'s multiscalar interactions amidst changes of transgender rights projects. Naghma's recounting of performances in *ilaka*s, to her staging with Lucky Khan a *vadhai* song "Balkada" ("Beloved Boy") for Coke Studio (2018b), Pakistan's largest music platform, illustrates the affective possibilities and struggles of *vadhai* within the shifting contexts of mainstreaming transgender citizens (see Introduction, p. 22–26). The popular lullaby "Balkara" of the *vadhai* repertoire, praising the birth of a boy, is remixed together with humorous lyrics of women mourning the loss of their own freedoms and pleasures, and Naghma's personal narrative of being thrown out of her home in childhood, fusing the bouncy notes and witty lyrics of Punjabi *tappa* with rap-like funk. Widely distributed through television and internet channels, "Balkada" reached horizontally, receiving many heart emojis from audiences in cities and villages in Pakistan, and across national borders of South Asia (Coke Studio 2018b). YouTube comments attested to the power of the song to rouse diverse emotions, with many telling it moved them to tears, smiles, goosebumps, dancing, and/or laughter (Coke Studio 2018b). For some it rekindled memories of *khwaja sira-hijra* performances at weddings and birth celebrations. Others found it demonstrative of the power of music to move beyond boundaries—whether of nation, religion, class, and/or gender (Coke Studio 2018b), and some praised a modern and progressive "naya [new] Pakistan" through its transgender representation.

Coke Studio's marketing of the song reveals some of the unfolding tensions around *vadhai* in Pakistan's transgender visibility projects. Its 2018 release, shortly after the passing of the Transgender Persons (Protection of Rights) Act,[2] just weeks following the national electoral win of Imran Khan's PTI (Pakistan Tehreek-e-Insaf) government with its promises of a "naya Pakistan," and days before the celebration of Pakistan and India's independence commemorations (14, 15 August, respectively), was clearly intended to harness progressivist nationalist sentiments. This is further amplified through the glossy advertisements promoting the "transgender debutant singers," alongside the multinational beverage logo and the season slogan: "One Nation, One Spirit, One Sound" (Coke Studio 2018a)—pointing to the intersecting logics of neoliberal globalization and nationalism in demarcating transgender citizenship. In a recorded interview, the elite cismen producers espouse these ideals, in the discourse of classist respectability, morality, and normative citizenship, typical of rights projects, telling Lucky and Naghma: "Our intention is to break the stereotype that has developed around here […] we want to show you as *normal people*" (my emphasis, Coke Studio 2018c). Naghma by contrast refuses assimilation into the normative, uplifting kinship practices that have been increasingly under attack amidst transgender movements, telling how her *guru* taught her the song in her *dera* after her birth family rejected her. As such, "Balkada" was unusual for bringing to a mainstream performance platform an item explicitly from the *vadhai* repertoire, cultivated through the *dera* and its lineage— attachments that are increasingly chastised as harkening to "stereotypes," or at worst denounced as "criminal mafias," "enslaving," or "Indian" structures, as I elaborate later. While the song helped propel Naghma and Lucky's recognition as singers, Naghma also returns power to the community, refusing to serve up an exceptional transgender narrative for the multinational corporation. She quipped in our conversations, "no matter how many Coca Colas they give us, vadhai will never end, this culture can't end. It's the staple of the dera system, khwaja siras depend on it" (Gogi 2019). This chapter traces out the sometimes contested movements of *vadhai*, in and across *dera*s, *ilaka*s, and national forums, to highlight these performances' multiplicitous registers, affects, and doings, as performers navigate multiscalar marginalizations undergirded by colonial legacies, post-colonial nationalism, and transgender rights and visibility projects.

An engagement with *vadhai* in motion offers a departure from the statism of structuralist approaches, which as we earlier note have often served to "straighten" these performances out. This verb comes from Sara Ahmed, whose affective investments, to "feel your way" (2004: 1), offer a useful prompt to engage with the more abundant possibilities of these performances in the realms of feelings. Through repertories woven through the *dera* lineage—themselves cultivated across interactions with *jajman* (patrons, lit. hosts) past and present—and in improvisation with particularities of the performance moment, *khwaja sira* performers build intimacies with each other and their publics, offering possible spaces for feelings—in ways that complicate narrow readings of these events' ritual procreative efficacy. Songs, dances, prayers, comedy, gesture, touch, shock, and spectacle, generate powerful emotions that move publics in different ways—sometimes to generosity, tears, laughter, into dance, and/or to hostility, or elsewhere. As Ahmed argues, bodies inhabit space through shared orientations (2006: 118) wherein "orientation is about making the strange familiar through the extension of bodies into space, [and] disorientation occurs when that extension fails" (11). While attentive to the pain and precarity of disorientation, (Introduction 29–30) through the violence of gender, sexuality, class, kinship, and religious hierarchies, I foreground *vadhai*'s movements and ultimately agency through structures that otherwise work systemically to limit *khwaja sira* bodies in space. *Khwaja sira* performers feel their way through shifting orientations of their publics *and* shift their orientations, however fleetingly. Their performances may lean in to their publics' orientations, push them to experience disorientations, and/or reorient hierarchical social arrangements. I trace such affective possibilities through careful performance analysis, inspired by scholarship foregrounding participatory and improvisatory performance in the Global South (Amine and Carlson 2012, 2008; Drewal 2003; Kapchan 1995, 2007, 2017; Taylor 2020) and draw from my collaborative theater, performance, and film work with *khwaja sira* performers, to center the intercorporeality of these events. In so doing, I hope to put into motion what Shroff explicates as affective *khwaja sira* worldmaking, "demonstrat[ive] that our existences are entangled with each other" (2020: 278). This chapter engages these affective entanglements, first by following the weaving of *vadhai*'s repertoires through several ensembles performing in different Punjabi *ilaka*s, and then exploring how these relationalities feel through national "territories," propelled by transgender rights of the last decade.

Weaving Affects in *Ilaka*s

A Dera

> I am going with the sehra [wedding garland and wedding song] to the door of Christ,
> I collect roses, jasmine and nature's buds.
> Like a gardener, I weave a sehra,
> I am going with the sehra to the door of Christ.
> [...]
> Allah's thread, and good deed's needle,
> Are strung together by Himself.
> Like a gardener, I weave a sehra,
> I am going with the sehra to the door of Christ.
>
> (Amber et al. 2019)

Guru Amber, in her well-kept *dera* in the lower-income area of Bhaghvanpura Lahore (yet untouched by mega-development projects), spontaneously started singing various items of the repertoire as she was cooking breakfast for her *toli* ensemble and my film team (working on what would become the film and live performance event *Vadhai: A Gift*).[3] She gestured her *mirasi* musicians into a casual rehearsal for the day's labor, an event common to many *dera*s, where performance is often embedded in day-to-day household workings (Pamment 2019a: 307; Roy 2016: 418). The music and smells of food burst into an adjacent bedroom where I and Anaya Rahimi—my *Teesri Dhun* collaborator and friend who introduced me to this group—were smoking and chatting with Amber's *chela*s Goshi, Sheela, and Maham—speeding up the tempo of their hair and make-up preparations. It was the end of Muharram (2019), the Shi'a period of mourning, and there were apprehensions about how publics would receive them today. While Muharram is acknowledged in a two-day holiday by the Islamic Republic of Pakistan where Sunni-Islam is dominant, their *toli* (like many others) had only just started performing after a month of pious hiatus. Shi'a beliefs and rituals are closely observed by many *toli*s (Pamment 2019a) who set aside a share of regular *vadhai* earnings (often 10 percent) to cover expenses in this period, and to host a *niaz* (community feast), which Amber had organized in the previous week for the *ilaka* and *khwaja sira* kin and friends. Amber further leaned into Shi'a sentiments, with a lively *qasida* (versified praises) in devotion to Hazrat Ali (an important figure in Shi'a Islam): "Sohna Lagda Ali Wala" ("Anyone Remembering Ali is Dear to Me"). Its energizing Punjabi beat—picked up by Shabbir on the *dholki* (drum) and Aamir on the *sheesha* (metal clappers), with impassioned vocals by Amber and the male musicians, awakened the entire house and seemed to lift the mood. Even the people in the household's upper portion (run by Amber's *bhateeja chela* or niece), responded with calls of "Ali Maula!" and one of their musicians came down, respectfully lay a 50 rupee note in front of Faisal (who sings and plays the harmonium), and joined the singing, raising the music's vigor. Amber continued this Shi'a devotion with "Nabi Say Pehlay Khuda" ("Before the Prophet is God"), in gliding notes, tracing the lineage from Allah, to the Prophet, his son-in-law Ali, his wife Fatima Zahra, to her sons Hassan and Hussain—whose tragic death at the Battle of Karbala is mourned in this holy month. Amber and the musicians felt out and shifted orientations of those in and around the space: the chatter quelled, the camera turned from talking heads and make-up to music-making, the household sounded out from above, the *chela*s began to help with chores, and the entire *dera* warmed up to the day's labor of *vadhai*.

As I began moving around the space, loading up equipment for my camera person, Amber moved into the wedding song, relayed above, with its Christian registers. While not sensed by me at the time as I fiddled with technology, it was in reviewing video footage that I saw Amber's eyes wander in my direction then back to the musicians, as though cueing the item in response to my presence. Whether she was working on the assumption in this first meeting of ours that I as a white woman might be Christian, or because weeks earlier I had expressed interest in learning about these minoritarian items of the repertoire from her *chela*s, the expectation was that I might find feeling in the song. This attempt to attune me into the performance is illustrative of *vadhai*'s tenacity to feel out those in the space, and a reminder that the researchers' embodied presence affects performance in different ways (see Introduction, p. 38–39). By extension, it gestures to how my own orientations shape my encounter with *vadhai*—here, my lack of any particular religious attachments and immediate preoccupations may have missed this moment, and point to the methodological im/possibilities of sensing *all* the cues and feelings circulating in these multilayered, multisensorial, and multiscalar improvisatory performances. Diana Taylor's discussion of other immersive performances are pertinent to *vadhai*: "There is no privileged or hegemonic spectator [...] who can evaluate and see everything [...] No frame or stage could contain it—it has too many moving parts" (2020: 218).

Like Taylor's "walking theory [of] thinking [and I would add, feeling] in and through the embodied and discursive acts of transfer" (2020: 9), or what Drewal describes as the "pleasures of experiencing improvisation" (2003: 119), I depart from epistemologies of objectivity in performance research, toward a privileging of proximities (Conquergood 2013), in moving through acts of transfer. In the *ilaka* performances I fluctuate between being with the group (wandering the streets with the *toli*, helping fasten the *ghungroo* ankle bells, taking prompts over what the *toli* or *jajman* want me to film, and being privy to internal cues and banter about publics, sometimes cultivated through my long-term relationships and performance collaborations with practitioners), and being with the *jajman* (standing in the crowd, throwing awards of *vail*, and often being moved to feeling through performances). Through my movings with performers and publics, I sense (however imperfectly, to borrow from Roy, p. 108) the reciprocal exchanges of these intercorporeal performances, while foregrounding how performers shape acts of transfer, and valorizing their own theorizations of these doings.

Amber's episode in her *dera* gestures to how she weaves temporal, spatial, embodied, and sensorial particularities, while drawing upon repertoires—expansive and pluralistic—accrued over the lineage, to generate the performance moment, draw people in, make place, and find feeling. While Islam often takes a central place in these performances, with *dera*s expressing Shi'a and Sufi affiliations as a group (Pamment 2019a), as Amber explained, she learnt Christian wedding songs through the lineage, given the presence of some Christian *chela*s, and Christian colonies within the *ilaka*. While *hijra*'s "supra" religious kinship practices, rituals, and oral histories are acknowledged (see Introduction, p. 9–10; Hossain 2012: 497–9; Reddy 2005: 100, 117, 120), *vadhai* extends understanding of *khwaja sira-hijra-trans* religious pluralities in relation to publics. *Vadhai* entails music and dance particular to the religious orientations of the *toli* and *ilaka* households. Performers might offer Shi'a

Muslims the wild corporealities of the *dhamaal* dance-prayer (Pamment 2019a: 306–7). To increasingly numerous orthodox Wahabi Muslims patrons—who often denounce performance and Sufi shrines—performers sometimes minimize song and dance and offer a *naat*, or even sing of Sufi saints. Or, as Amber reveals in the *sehra* performed at Christian households, performers might bring together different religious registers, here Islam and Christianity. Figuring herself as the needle of Allah's good deeds and a gardener, she weaves the *sehra* (the wedding song and garland) to take to the door of Christ. Weaving, needlework, and spinning are metaphors particularly pronounced across Punjabi repertoires, gesturing to women's labor, Sufi spirituality, and the work of creating from—and for—a diverse social fabric. The registers of Sunni-dominant Pakistani nationalism often has a tenuous relationship with Sufism, and marginalizes Shi'a, Christian, and other minoritarian faith communities, but Amber's performances suggest how pluralistic religious registers mingle in *khwaja sira*' affective worldmaking. I continue to follow repertoires in performers' weaving—as well as through their already woven presence—in their *ilaka*s.

An *Ilaka*

Before sending Goshi out to lead the *toli* for the day, *Guru* Amber told me: "Those houses known to our ancestors give respect, in newer areas where people don't know us they can insult us a lot." Stepping out of the lane of the *dera*, Goshi navigated our path in search of births and weddings, across the bazaar and meandering small lanes, heels dodging potholes, *dholki*s edging traffic, and the group interacting with the smiles and stares of passersby. A shopkeeper gave away a few *samosa*s (like the movements across *cholla* and *badhai* of Hossain's chapter), elsewhere a uniformed school boy derisively clapped at the performers, a man almost fell off his bicycle while gawking at the group, a young shirtless man leaned flirtatiously out of his doorway, and an old bearded man reached for Goshi's head in a paternal gesture of respect. Many women stopped to chat and share *ilaka* gossip, some inviting us into their homes, while the male musicians and camera person were served water outside. Though Goshi had only been initiated in the *ilaka* the previous year, after decades of working as an invited dancer in *functions* (typically male only events), without prior experience of *vadhai*, women residents were particularly welcoming, apparently relishing a break from household labor. They engaged in banter, while serving to me and Anaya affectionate anecdotes of Goshi's *guru*s, sometimes extending back to her great grand *guru*. As the senior *chela* to Amber, she is next in line to inherit the *ilaka*—not only the physical geographical areas where this *toli* performs, but the relationships developed with *jajman* over the lineage. Goshi in turn brings her own personality and skills to these relationships, known in the *khwaja sira* community for her sharp wit, qualities clearly cherished in the *ilaka*. In one exchange, a woman popped out of her doorway to give her respects to Goshi and enquire who I was. Goshi pulled me close and playfully told her that I was a new member of the troupe, making fun of rigid identity demarcations, to a friendly laugh of delight from the woman. In another street, a masculine presenting person stopped to chat, telling of their new marriage. While we turned to go on our way, Sheela whispered that they were actually a *khwaja sira* stumbling through heteronomative family constraints. Sheela, the youngest of the group, had recently become *Guru* Amber's *chela*, and while quiet in the *dera*, was bold and often tactile in her interactions with people on the street: making place for herself and her performance in the *ilaka*, which increases *izzat* (respect) and belonging in the *dera* (Roy 2015a: 11–13). She describes first finding community with another group of *khwaja sira* performers in her village on their *toli* rounds, a refuge from the violence of her birth home, and analogized her own experience of performing *vadhai* to building extended family, within the *toli* and within the *ilaka*: "we don't have our own families, but when we go out we find all kinds of relationships, they [the *jajman*] are like our family."

While *jajman* are denoted by *toli* groups as *dunyadar* ("people of the world"), the entangled relationalities with *jajman* extend lineage. The rounds of banter strengthen bonds within *khwaja sira* kinship, keep connections alive with the neighbors, and importantly point paths to new births, weddings and new residents in the area.

Despite these zones of familiarity, as Amber gestured— and Hossain makes clear in the shifting urban geographies of Dhaka (p. 52)—*ilaka*s are never stable entities. Old building structures may be dismantled and new ones built up, nuclear family structures supplant joint ancestral households, original inhabitants move and newcomers enter, and financial economies and relations change with time, offering no guarantee of patronage. At a time of steep inflation, after over two hours of laboring our way in the sweltering sun, with only a 100 rupee note (about 60 cents) from a welcoming but impoverished mother of a newborn girl, Goshi decided to spend her hard-earned rupees on a rickshaw fare to a village within her *ilaka*, a 20-minute ride away. Her informant, a young boy, had called to say that a son had been born there. Upon arrival, she first checked in on a few houses to gather what she could about the family who were not known to her, while generating a captive audience who followed her to the house. Since her customary laudations in the name of Allah, "Bismillah," had prompted a rude response by the father of a newborn, who appeared only briefly to shoo the group away, Goshi bellowed out loud in the open street: "Has he just moved into this area?" She asserted her relations with the neighbors over his, causing him to shrink back into the house. With a quick flick of her wrist, she gestured Maham and Sheela to follow him inside, while the musicians set instruments on the pavement, and offered a prelude of Muslim devotional songs to sustain the growing crowd and draw others in. Inside, enraged at the intrusion, the householder fiercely reprimanded the group in a middle-class bourgeois assertion of personal property: "If there is a burglary in our house we will blame you," correlating the group with criminality and extortion, a trope familiar to the colonial archive. Goshi was sharp in her rebuttal, claiming spiritual legitimacy through the Sufi *faqir*'s renunciation of the worldly and proximities to Allah (Pamment 2019a): "This is our vadhai. We are faqirs. We can take the vadhai. We have been faqirs from the start of time. Now bring the boy out and let us give the lullaby." Drawing powers from the lineage across (and beyond) normative temporalities, and pushing religiously imbued ethical thresholds, she trivializes the householder's privatization of property and asserts her right to *vadhai*.

To further sustain the throng of onlookers, Goshi signaled Maham and Sheela to begin dancing at his door. Useful in thinking through *vadhai*'s intercorporealities and place-making is *al-halqa* (the circle) of Moroccan performance with legacies in Arab-Islamic cultures wherein: "The interdependence between performer and audience is implicit [...]; neither exists without the other, making all who are present coparticipants" (Kapchan 1995: 485; Amine and Carlson 2008: 72–4; 2012). The *toli*'s dance and music anchors publics into a circular formation of proximities, and set the stage for the reluctant householder to participate by performing his generosity and prestige, or failing under his neighbors' gaze. He complied, handing over the baby. Goshi rocked the child while singing the aforementioned lullaby "Balkara," which typically weaves all gathered family members into its lyrics and they respond with showerings of *vail*, but here there were no extended family, nor did the father give anything. This prompted playful verbal lacerations from Goshi: "Are you sure this kid is yours? You are so white and the kid is not!" Goshi debunked his fair skin (normatively socially desirable) to question the child's paternity and father's virility—rubbing against patriarchy, whiteness/colorism, and markers of class, to the great amusement of the crowd. The man nervously laughed along, edging a 1,000 rupees note ($6) to the performers (see Figure 7). This was not enough, as Goshi made clear, now loudly lambasting the man to the circle of neighbors about the low value he had placed on his son, causing the householder to again attempt escape. The musicians began to reorient the palpable tensions by lifting

FIGURE 7 *Goshi challenging the reluctant householder's low award of vail (top left), calling out his miserliness to the neighbors (top right), and Sheela and Maham coaxing him into their dance (below). Stills from the film Vadhai: A Gift (Pamment et al. 2019c).*

the beat of their music into a lively film number, as Sheela and Maham whirled toward the householder, and playfully pulled him into the circle. His hands came out of his pockets, throwing notes, and he danced along Punjabi *bhangra*-style with the performers. Drawing from the already woven connections with familiar *jajman* in the *ilaka*, coupled with agile improvisations, the *toli* shifts the householder's orientations. Witty puns and verbal jousts both pinpoint and unhinge his assertions of property, class and cisheteropatriarchy. The lure of music and dance bring movement to the householder's rigidity, rechoreographing his body, reorienting him, compelling him to participate—momentarily shifting hierarchies, opening up bodies, wallets, and spaces, transforming fear into pleasure and distance to proximity.

Public Intimacies

In what follows I further dwell in such proximities as they transpire among (often) more willing *jajman*, in journeys with different *toli* groups, in various areas of Lahore, and across a range of scales and sensorial interactions. In the process I hope to further complicate narrow definitions of ritual procreative efficacy, beyond what has been described of a *hijra*'s blessings to a male son "giving to him what she does not possess: the power of creating new life, of having many sons, and of carrying on the continuity of his family line. [...] It is this role that defines their identity to the world around them" (Nanda [1990] 1999: 3), or more flagrantly as "help[ing] expand the nectar of the man" (Saria 2021: 58). I borrow insights from Omar Kasmani, who, while writing in different contexts of Sufi *zikr* circles in Berlin, explores the permeability of intimate interiority with publicness, as possibilities for bending the normative social order (2021b: 195). While *vadhai* invariably announces key cisheteronormative milestones to the larger community, these performances in and around emotionally charged heteronormative ritual events of weddings and births may feel beyond these structures, or what Kasmani calls "elsewhere" by "cit[ing] shared desires and anxieties of its participants" (Kasmani 2021b: 189; Kasmani et al. 2020; see Roy, p. 113). Moments of intimacy—from the familial to the erotic—produced through music, dance, and humor, give participants the possibilities to feel "elsewhere", which may, however fleetingly, reorient cisheteropatriarchal and other social orderings.

Vadhai, even in the *ilaka*, operates on a spectrum of scales, from big gatherings where *jajman* often show off their male heirs to extended family and neighbors, through to smaller more private events. A *vadhai* led by Nanni—Anaya's *chacha guru* (lit. uncle *guru*) in the Mozang area of Lahore (October 2019), entailed a sprawling crowd, corresponding to the multi-generational relationships with the *toli* across the family's patrilineal line, as the grandma proudly announced by introducing me to her grandsons, nephews, brothers, and sons, whose births had all been celebrated by this *khwaja sira* lineage. Here, the item "Balkara" took full force, weaving all family members into the inner circle of performance who in turn issued generous rewards of *vail*: "The moon-like child is receiving the lullabies, with good wishes the mother gives you the lullaby, the father is giving gifts, you have a long life!" Anaya, a skilled actor-deviser who I directed in *Teesri Dhun*, and is a versatile stand-up comedienne, was assisting me in research while waiting news from a corporate job interview, and was now performing *vadhai* for the first time. The *jajman* welcomed her as a new member of the *toli*, and an extension of their family, urging her to perform her own specialty items, and pulling her over for a chat. Despite the accent on male heirs, and the heterogeneous composition of the gathering, the older aunties took full reign in shouting out their favorite music requests and beckoning us over to their plastic chairs for Coca-Colas, jokes, and photos—apparently feeling through their own pleasures. After an exhausting but well-compensated two hours, we moved on—following a middle-aged woman who had been quietly chatting with Nanni, to a discreet adjoining lane. There, the woman held the hand of a young man—an unusual display of affection in public space—and the *toli* offered a brief set, dancing to a *sehra*, with a film song on request. A young girl, who kept interrupting my filming to tell me how beautiful Anaya was, informed me that the woman was marrying again—certainly not taboo, but on the edges of the social radar. As such, moments of intimacies spin out from even large public events.

These performances can engender a plurality of intimacies, as Reema Jaan and her *chela* Sana made clear through two *vadhai* performances that Reema invited me to in Nishtar Colony, Lahore (2014). An accomplished dancer, Reema had at the time only recently returned to *vadhai* after dancing in the Punjabi theater, circus, and at a bar in Kuwait, explaining that in *vadhai* she felt a freedom from "passing." One house initially refused to open its doors, yet with Reema and her *chela*'s persistent dancing on the streets, an eager audience soon gathered—making place for performance—and stirring the householders to participate (see Introduction, see p. 1). Three brothers were getting married, which generated a largely male gathering, along with their mother and sisters on the street. They all seemed to relish in the tactile interaction with the dancers, putting cash notes over each others' heads—and mine—and not releasing them till Reema or Sana had kissed their/my cheeks, shaking up and teasing out sexual possibilities, in flirtatious play. In another household to celebrate the birth of a son, after singing the *lori*, Reema offered a diverse set, from devotional *naat*, the head turning Sufi-Shi'a *dhamaal*, to the erotic *filmi* snake dance's gyrations (see Figure 8). The middle-aged women laughed and reveled in the erotic dance numbers of pulsating chests and swinging hips. Then, adjusting her *dupatta* (scarf) modestly over her head, Reema sang of women's rites of passage, with the refrain: "Mothers are the cool shades [of trees]"—stirring several of the women to tears, prompting Reema to extend comfort, reaching out and touching their heads in a climatic

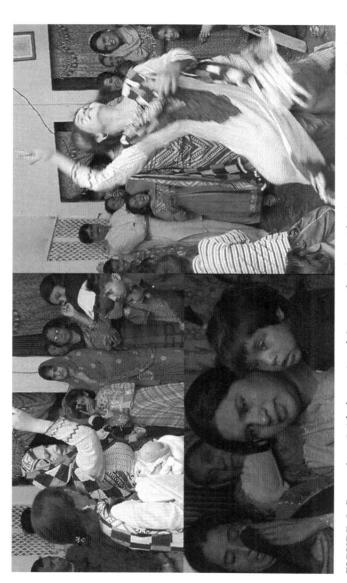

FIGURE 8 *Reema Jaan (with dupatta) and Sana performing with jajman, generating tears and laughter, Lahore, 2014 (Photo: Hamza Abbas Malik).*

emotional encounter of contact (Pamment 2019a: 307–8). Reema reflected on this intercorporeal exchange, explaining that the item makes both men and women remember their mothers, "it centres the mother, she is number one of the house" (Reema 2019). For some women who have left their birth homes upon marriage, this entails a particular sense of loss and sadness—making empathic connections with *khwaja sira* performers who have often been forced out of their birth homes by heteropatriarchal conventions (Pamment 2019a: 308). Such performances of mournful emotionality through to cheeky sexual flirtations, generate sensual and intimate experiences of tears, kisses, and laughter—gesturing entangled relations of shared anxieties, histories, and desires, "elsewheres" that may reorient the heteropatriarchal focus of the celebratory event.

Further reorienting possibilities are amplified in the *charkha* (lit. spinning wheel), sometimes presented at the end of a set: a comic *tappa* song/verbal skit, punctuated by *dholki* beats on the punchlines, and physical play.[4] Anmol Shah Bukhari (AB) from Sahiwal and Ashee Jee (A) of Raiwind, Lahore (who I introduce further in the next section)—each of the same lineage but different *deras*—offered a *charkha* episode that was known to them both, over tea at my house (Bukhari and Ashee 2019). Similar to Punjabi *sithni*s that comically depict women's journeys from marriage to childbirth, performed often by women wedding celebrants at weddings (Batool 2004), *charkha* plays a comic pantomime of women's labor, motherhood, and wifedom, with a bawdy mime of working the spinning wheel, through to breastfeeding a pretend baby of rolled-up *dupatta*, in pacey Punjabi repartee:

AB Don't hit him! It's a bundle of chiffon. He'll be torn!

A But he's a pest!

AB   Why?

A   He wants both tits.

AB   Why don't you give him both?

A   No! I told him one is for you, and the other is for the father, that letch!

AB   What's the name of the boy's father?

A   I don't take his name without respect.

AB   What is his profession?

A   The father dresses up all the dogs on the railway station, with underwear.

AB   What's the name of the mother?

A   Oh, I have so many names.

AB   Tell us them all!

A   My name is Silai Walli, the one who stitches.

AB   Wow, I have come to a prosperous house with milk and a son! What's your second name?

A   Karma Walli, the Fortunate One. Wherever I go, I pray for them.

AB   What's your third name?

A   Sarhana, the Pillow. I have to be in the house with the son, and give milk.

AB   What's your fourth name?

A   No, I'm not going to tell you! I'm called that name by my husband, only he knows.

AB   Oh my god! What name is that?

A   Oh, I'm feeling very shy!

AB   Please tell us!

A   Well, all day long he calls me bitch, bitch, bitch!
       (Bukhari and Ashee 2019)

Anmol initiated this episode after highlighting the special
interaction that unfolds between *khwaja sira* performers
and women householders, telling me, "Sister. We mostly deal
with the women [...] people's sisters and mothers are like
our own, we really respect women," or as some *khwaja sira*
performers elaborate of these emotional entanglements: "we
feel like women feel." "Feeling" women in the *charka*, plays
amock with the cyclic drudgery of heteronormative married
life, and pokes patriarchy. If the *khwaja sira* performers stand
apart from these structures and mock them, so too do *jajman*
in the shared laughter such sequences often elicit. In a typical
ending—though this too weaves with the particularities of
the occasion—performers chase after the little boys in the
gathering, as if to tickle their genitals, taunting them for their
"little snakes." A structuralist analysis might read this moment
as a restoration of patriarchy, urging boys to manhood; Anmol
and Ashee instead describe the act through feeling, as the "fun
finale," making a commotion with sensorial giddiness, which
disperses bodies in space and elicits laughter—generating
glee and further shaking up bodily boundaries of these
intercorporeal events. Here, like other elements of *vadhai*'s
repertoires, the weavings, stitchings, and spinnings are left as
loose threads, for each individual participant—in themselves
and with each other—to feel their way through.

Paths Back to *Dera*s

Anmol asserts, "Our biggest weapon is our toli." Just as *toli*s
weave relationalities within *ilaka*s, the acts of making and
sharing music, choreographies, and humor collaboratively

entail possibilities for weaving relationalities in *khwaja sira* kinship, in and beyond *dera*s (see Introduction, p. 6). The *dera*—while for some may entail its own violence and hierarchies—often serves as a refuge from "unhomely" natal families (Hamzić 2019). *Vadhai* may cultivate self-expression and strengthen kinship bonds of the *dera*, through embodied ways of knowing and doing, passed down through the lineage of community elders or *guru*s. One *Chaudhry* elaborates,

> We have to see where we are going. We can only do that from our gurus' experiences. Other khwaja siras coming just to beg don't know who is who. They will never know who is Shi'a, Wahabi, Christian [...] I know because I live with these people. My gurus have been going to their houses. Everything requires time. We are not arriving there for the first time.

While the assertion of *ilaka* territories enables performers to navigate relationalities in *dera*s and *ilaka*s, it may also delineate others to these relations—here named "*khwaja sira* beggars." Like the *birit bakhor* Hossain discusses, *ilaka* territorial disputes have been well documented in literature for re/inscribing "real"/"fake" dichotomies (Dutta 2012; Reddy 2005: 206), particularly around axes of bodily authenticity and demarcations of *hijra/zenana* identities (Nanda [1990] 1999: 11–12)—each part of the *khwaja sira* spectrum with separate but sometimes affiliated kinships (Pamment forthcoming b). My turn to the affective investments of *ilaka*s aims to complicate such binaries, while highlighting the contested and shifting edges of *ilaka* territories—which around my 2019 research often coalesced with discourse around transgender rights, with its sentiments against "begging" and *dera*s.

While *dera*s have endured recent denouncements as "enslaving structures," or are sometimes defended through strategic essentialist definitions of piety and purity—each entail workings as diverse as the individuals that constitute them, reflected in the composition of their *toli*s. The *toli*s of this chapter often cut across normative hierarchies of class, gender, religion, and labor, and frequently integrate individuals with varying attachments to their *dera*s, from permanent residents to those who live with their birth families and/or are engaged in other work. As such, while Amber has lived in the *dera* since her youth and has only worked in *toli*s, her *nati chela* Maham lives with her birth family and has a full-time job as a field officer for an MSM organization, working *toli* intermittently. Maham states that after her salary was suspended due to donor delays, and the MSM office asked her to stop *firka* (feminine dress), *toli* has provided material safety, self-expression, and facilitated kinship bonds: "I got so much appreciation, from my gurus and the *jajman* [who told me] 'you dance so well!' [...] I started thinking of myself as a mashuq [darling]" (in Pamment 2019c). In turn, *toli*s may extend beyond these immediate kinships through inter-/intra-community assemblages that span performers affiliated in *hijra* and/or *zenana* lineages. Neeli Rana, a *zenana Chaudhry* who doesn't have a *rit* or formal affiliation in *hijra* lineages (though some *zenana*s do), but has performed with *dera toli*s, assigns political power to the complexly woven affective lineages of this collaborative art. Critiquing the individualizing impulses of neoliberal transgender rights paradigms, she provocatively asks: "from where did the protests start? By knocking at peoples' doors, and going out in the streets! [...] In *toli* we share our earnings. One person cannot take away all the money, all the glory." (in Pamment et al. 2021: 222). Neeli probes us to consider the possibilities and limitations of these assemblages in entering new national "territories," which don't necessarily entail the specific *ilaka* attachments cultivated through *dera* lineages. In the following section I engage *vadhai*'s affective movements in and around national/ist "territorializations" of transgender inclusion.

National Territories

Almas Bobby, who in 2009 steered protests against the arrests of *khwaja sira* dancers that roused the Supreme Court to hearings of human rights violations against *khwaja sira* people (Pamment 2019b), appeared a year later as a *toli* leader, collecting not *vadhai* but taxes from the mansions of corrupt government elite in a parody song on Geo TV's popular political sketch show *Hum Sab Umeed se Hain* (*We Are All Pregnant*, January 9, 2010, in Ahmad Murtaza 2010). The song came on the heels of an announcement by the Sindh government to employ *khwaja sira* people as tax collectors (following similar measures in Patna, India), after the Supreme Court had instructed civil society and government agencies that "steps be made to create some respectable jobs so that they may earn their livelihood respectably" (Supreme Court 2009). The Supreme Court implied that *khwaja sira* occupations, particularly performance and "begging", were unrespectable and to blame for the social violence inflicted upon them; redemption was through reform to so-called "respectable" citizens, or what an adjoining report defines as employment in "socially useful work" (Supreme Court 2009). These reformist aspirations into middle-class moral economies of "respectable" and "useful citizenship" follow the recuperative logics imposed upon various other South Asian performers marginalized by nationalist projects (see Introduction, p. 16).

Hum Sab Umeed se Hain plays havoc with these government scriptings, drawing on *vadhai*'s reorienting possibilities. The camera pans to a lavish residence with its signboard "Sugar Mills"—an industry that had recently attracted media headlines for its rampant corruption, by politicians and their kin (Cheema 2009). Bobby's red nail-polished finger pushes the door bell, causing the house itself to tremble in fear, as the group loudly sing congratulations, but here the laudations to a newborn child (*"baccha hua!"*) are replaced with a eulogy to the birth of national debt ("*karza hua!*"). The noise brings a minister out of his house, his hands firmly planted in his pockets, reluctant to part with his wealth, as the *toli* group, waving tax forms in their hands, sing, "What skills we have in our hands that we can collect the tax!" These skills of *vadhai* cause the flustered minister to attempt an escape in his car, but his tyres, like his persona, are punctured by the *toli* as he stands outside on the street, exposed for tax evasion. The *khwaja sira* performers prove inescapable. They haunt another minister from the back of his classy Corolla car. They erupt from under a politician's dining table at an elite restaurant, serenading him to dance. They jump out of a businessman's expensive LCD TV and into his pocket, and re-emerge dancing on banknotes. Finally, all of these high-status male identities dissemble, as they run as though for their lives, with the *toli* group hounding behind. Like *jajman* of *ilaka* performances who participate in the spectacular redress of those who refuse to share wealth and space, television audiences are invited to laugh along *with* the performers, at their exposés of elite governmental corruption. While the imaging strays from *vadhai*'s multiplicitous affects in *ilaka*s, and also from the realities of *khwaja sira* people actually employed in tax collecting positions—it gestures to understandings of *vadhai*'s possibilities in national politics.[5]

Considering the agility of repertoires in shifting orientations, it is no surprise to find practitioners themselves using *vadhai* to engage the national discourse on *khwaja sira*-transgender rights. However, while these collective modes defined how several *khwaja sira* people secured public sentiment in national forums in the early phases of rights projects (Pamment 2019a), over time this has been less so, as the Supreme Court, legislature, and NGOs have increasingly blamed "enslaving" community structures, "begging," and performance practices for infringing upon the respect, rights and freedom of *khwaja sira* people (Pamment forthcoming b). Tracing brief appearances of *vadhai* within dominant circulations, in the national elections of 2013 and around the passing of the Transgender Persons Act of 2018, I foreground how *vadhai* weaves affect by feeling in, against, and across increasingly classist, religious, and neoliberal nationalist orientations.

Centering *Vadhai* in the National Elections (2013)

Khwaja sira candidates contesting the 2013 elections, amongst several others, included Sanam Faqir from Sindh and Hajji Nargis from Multan who actively drew their long experiences of performing *vadhai* into their campaigns, bringing concerns from their *ilaka* constituents to the polls. Sanam Faqir, a focal person in the Supreme Court judgment for *khwaja sira* people, and familiar with the government's scripts of "useful citizenship," weaves these registers in a television interview during the lead up to elections, asserting, "It is not our destiny to merely dance for others and hold begging bowls" (in AFP 2013). While leaning into the state's anti-performance and anti-begging discourse, she explains how she actively brought *vadhai* into her campaign with an election symbol of a baby cot, and working through affect cultivated in her *ilaka*:

> We would go door to door. See, this is what we already do, we go to people's celebrations. We are the symbol of happiness. So wherever we would go we would meet men or women of that house […] We would explain to them that since we never have children, so who would we do corruption for, or make huge property or anything for? So think about it and give us one chance.
>
> (Faqir 2014)

Hajji Nargis similarly placed herself above the corruption of other candidates, asserting her proximity to Allah through *vadhai*'s *faqiri* tropes and feeling through the concerns of underrepresented minoritarian groups:

These thugs, these hooligans, they think the vote is their property and they own it. These politicians rule the poor, as if they are gods. They become the MNAs [Members of the National Assembly] and MPAs [Members of the Provincial Assembly], but they have never helped the people who have made them those rulers. Allah will ask them if they supported the poor, the widows, the disabled; no, all they did was to make their own huge palaces and they spent all their money to fulfill their own needs... I am a faqir and that is what I ask for them, that Allah will one day question them.

(in Pamment 2019a: 310)

Nargis appears in a television interview on Samaa TV (2013) inbetween a segment where the general public speaks derisively of *khwaja sira*s in politics ("it's not possible" or "they will only bring song and dance") and a Mufti (Muslim legal expert) who is asked to judge if the *khwaja sira* politicians are *halal*, or legitimate in Islam; only a few months earlier, he had accused the *khwaja sira* community of being satanic (Pamment 2019a: 309). She reorients the derision and abjection by emphasizing the popular belief of *khwaja sira* people's ability to deliver *bad-dua* (lit. bad prayers or curse)—a performance mode of redress sometimes used when *khwaja sira* people are not treated well (Pamment 2010: 47–8).[6] Through dominant religious imagery of the Day of Judgment, she summons divine wrath on the politics of exclusion: "It is the system of Allah. Where there is no khawaja sira there will be problems. We are part of Pakistan. If we are not there will be earthquakes and floods. We are part of Pakistan. Those who don't think us part of this society and do not accept us, do not accept Allah!" (in Pamment 2019a: 310). On the TV show, she successfully reorients the Mufti, who nods in agreement and says he would himself vote for Hajji if he were in her constituency. Upon securing the Mufti's approval, she proceeds to beat her chest rhythmically like the *matam* or *sine-zani* of minoritarian

Shi'a Muharram rituals, similar to the protesting *khwaja sira*s who had roused the Supreme Court's attention to rights violations, tactics sometimes deployed by *khwaja sira* people to push ethical-affective thresholds in *ilaka*s when they are not respectfully welcomed to a birth or wedding (Pamment 2019a; 2019b). Nargis protests against the political status quo: "Politicians haven't done anything for the last fifty years except drones and wars, there is no electricity, everyone is fed up [... these politicians] should come and take answers from me" (Pamment 2019a: 309). She explains her political strategies through the emotional bonds woven in the *ilaka*: "We go to every house and we know what people's problems are. But those politicians; say for example, the one from this constituency does not know that this mother has lost her son, and the child is in the world without his father, but we do" (Pamment 2019a: 308). While these labors were not enough to win either Nargis nor Sanam seats, they certainly seemed to further secure feeling in their *ilaka*s when they returned to *vadhai*. During one of these performances, one *jajman* explained to me: "She participates in our weddings, funerals. Hajji sahib is different from the other [politicians] ... who come and meet people only to get votes. Hajji sahib ... is a part of our lives" (Pamment 2019a). These entangled existences signal political possibilities, nourished through *vadhai*.

Reddy warns how *hijra* projections of asexuality can slip into dangerous "real"/"fake" dichotomies and play into far-right religious nationalism, in analyzing *hijra* strategies in Indian elections of the early 2000s (2003: 187). Sanam and Nargis arguably resist these impulses, drawing upon their *ilaka* relations and in the process reorienting the dominant religious, classist, ableist, patriarchal, and economic hierarchies of the dominant political elite. While they may be seen to affirm the logics of "useful citizenship," both have continued to perform *vadhai*. Their electoral efforts, coupled with launching *vadhai*-funded social welfare initiatives in their *ilaka*s, have further bolstered their prestige and empathies with publics, in turn expanding the compass of their *dera*s. In what follows, I explore these and other movements of *vadhai* around the shifting discourses that accompany the Transgender Persons (Protection of Rights) Act (2018). Despite its capacious definition of transgender, the act inscribes Islamic laws of inheritance and property rights—negating non-Muslim *khwaja sira* and trans people, and names anyone who employs a transgender person for "begging" a criminal offence (Redding 2019: 2)—which could potentially criminalize forms of kinship and *vadhai*. While I don't dwell on these legal provisions, in highlighting moments of *vadhai*'s movings on the edges of transgender rights reforms, performance may further obfuscate any linear teleology of progressive rights—and too of any linear movement of *vadhai*—encouraging us to engage with a plurality of *vadhai*'s affective entanglements.

On the Edges of Transgender Rights Reforms (2018)

"For the first time in Pakistan's history, transgender citizens are contesting the elections," reported international NGO supporters of these candidates, ahead of the 2018 elections (Oxfam in Pakistan 2018). This celebration of "transgender firsts," while technically correct after the passing of the Transgender Persons Act in May 2018, marked a clear separation from the prior *khwaja sira* candidacy of Hajji Nargis and Sanam Faqir, rendering the activist labor of these and other *toli khwaja sira* politicians invisible. The transgender activist Nayyab Ali, contesting from Okara (NA 141) in a forum with constituents and the media, explained: "khwaja siras are perceived as uneducated, who can only beg and dance. I want to change this" (May 27, Samaa). Nadeem Kashish, another well-publicized candidate, contesting from Islamabad, and a prominent voice against the *guru-chela* "system," calling it exploitative and oppressive (Boone 2016), urged voters to "give the vote, not the note" (Igualdad 2018), to end the culture of begging, dancing, and sex work under *khwaja sira guru*s. As mentioned earlier, *guru-chela* kinship may entail violence for some, and the candidates may have their own painful experiences of these assemblages. Yet these activists, supported by the international NGO, arguably emboldened public feeling against these practices, suggesting *guru-chela* kinship, performance, sex work and "begging" to be anathema to the nation. Efforts to isolate these elements were equally pronounced in the aftermath of elections—where news erupted in NGO/activist circles that one donor had allegedly declared that *khwaja sira* people associated with *guru-chela* lineages would no longer qualify for funding (Iqbal 2018). The devalorization of *vadhai*'s labor works in tandem with these anti-*guru* sentiments, and is symptomatic of marginalizations in the project of transgender rights and circulations of donor capital. As I, and other scholars note, such "progress" of Pakistan's transgender rights, gestures to other structural inequities that come to be sedimented, including the privileging of some ways of gender nonconformity over others (Kasmani 2021a: 108; Pamment 2019b; Redding 2019: 108–12), which as we explicate in the introduction frames a "good/bad transgender" binary, which reinforces hierarchies along lines of class, caste, language, religion, kinship, and nation.

Nadeem Kashish—contesting against Imran Khan himself—did not win a political seat, but the candidacy arguably brought them and their Islamabad-based organization Saffar, which purports to work for transgender and *khwaja sira* rights, renewed media visibility. Their media campaigns have increasingly targeted *guru-chela* kinship, the flows of donor circulation, and the Transgender Persons Act—all of which they claim to be against the nation state and unIslamic. In one video, they call on "our hero" Prime Minister Imran Khan to criminalize *guru-chela* kinship, labeling it—similar to colonial taxonomies—as "trafficking," the "guru mafia," and generating panic about "gurus" being of Hindu origin, and signifying an Indian incursion to the freedom and security of the Islamic nation state (Trans News

2021c). Perhaps to defend the *dera* amidst these attacks, a small number of *guru*s have participated in Saffar's crusades, particularly against donor circulations and the Transgender Act, sometimes drawing upon *vadhai* in the process. One such campaign was a press conference with Kashish and a table of approximately seven *guru*s in January 2020, in response to the Prime Minister's launch of a new health provision eligible to all registered transgender people under the National Database & Registration Authority (Dawn 2019). While shifting categories of identification have remained productively ambiguous and legally open-ended since *khwaja sira*–transgender rights first entered the Supreme Court in 2009 (Khan 2019: 1158–9), Khan's health provision signaled that registration was necessary if *khwaja sira—trans* people were to access state welfare. His address to the new beneficiaries of, "our government is owning you" (Dawn 2019), likely raised concern about biopolitical control in the context of colonial histories of such processes (Redding 2021). The *khwaja sira guru*s at the press conference expressed anxiety about schemes of registration, where the transgender designation of "X" on passports, like NGO funding preoccupations, was seen to harness transgender identities within sexual health schemes and global LGB projects, associations that would threaten their respect in the *ilaka* (in Kashish 2020a; 2020b)—similar to concerns expressed by Bangladeshi communities (see Hossain's chapter). They asserted that they were woven into the fabric of their communities, carrying long religio-cultural lineages and *izzat* they felt were woefully maligned in the rights movement. Some offered a plea for their inclusion, such as *Guru* Arzoo who pledged, "we are not against anyone," but "please show this too," positioning *vadhai* and *khwaja sira* community lineages as inclusive: "we accept people from all religions" (in Kashish 2020a). Others were more exclusive, such as one *guru* who situated *vadhai* within a discourse of hyper-religious nationalism, blaming a "Jewish and British" foreign cultural onslaught through the transgender category, that pitted the NGO beneficiaries of new rights as sinful, corrupt, and doped by foreign influences (in Kashish 2020b)—orienting toward the most conservative Wahabi-inflicted sentiments.

By spring 2021, even *Guru* Arzoo leaned into such exclusivity, after her *dera* in Islamabad-Rawalpindi had been allegedly ransacked. In media interviews, she blamed this act on "beggars" or "fake khwaja siras"—abject tropes that have been on the rise around the Supreme Court's legislative upheavals (Pamment forthcoming b). *Guru* Arzoo worked these orientations to critique the Transgender Persons Act, for letting in "gays, lesbos [sic.] and beggars [sic.] who dress up for meetings and take all of our funds" (Trans News 2021b)—capitalizing on the continued criminalization of homosexuality and begging. She blamed these "Others" for attacking her *dera* and ruining the respect she has earned in the *ilaka*. Positioning *vadhai* as exemplary of her Islamic piety and inscribed in heteronormative ends, she pledged she was joining Nadeem Kashish and others in challenging the Transgender Persons Act in the Shariat Court for being unIslamic, against its clauses of self-determined gender identity (Trans News 2021a). Writing at a time when the Transgender Persons Act is being challenged in the Federal Shariat Court (December 2020–) of undecided fate, such leanings into the emotional appeal of religious nationalism in apparent defense of the *dera*, while concerning for a spectrum of gender nonconforming people, do not necessarily foreclose futurities. Bhattacharya, writing about the tide of religious nationalism in and around Indian *hijra* communities, warns that meta-narratives of religious nationalism "risk [...] the danger of missing out on the micro-narratives of resistance and protests emerging from within India's transgender movements that disrupt any singular narrative of transgender individuals performing nationalism to seek citizenship rights" (2019: 19). Similarly, the territorializations around *vadhai* in these particular dominant scalar interactions that play out in the capital city and its institutions of power, do not necessarily dictate the work of *vadhai* in the more intimate scales of the *ilaka* (as I have demonstrated), or elsewhere—weaving affect through different subjectivities, relationalities, and/or in different times and places.

Rather than working against the pulse of transgender rights and the onslaught of NGOs, a burgeoning number of *khwaja sira* performers have used *vadhai* to sustain their own intersectional social justice initiatives, in tangible material ways. These include, but are not limited to, the aforementioned Sanam Faqir and Hajji Nargis who run schools for impoverished children in their *ilaka*s. Anmol Bukhari runs Zindagi Welfare Society in Sahiwal, working trans-feminist advocacy against rape and sexual violence, describing herself as a "voluntary activist"—receiving funds not from donor agencies, but supporting her activism from *vadhai* income and knowledge networks. Similarly, Ashee Butt has used her earnings from *vadhai* to set up Beghar Foundation, a home for elderly *khwaja sira* people on the outskirts of Lahore. She asserts,

> I have made this from my own pocket, while other khwaja siras are travelling abroad [...] this is from doing sehra and lori. Those people [i.e. the *jajman*] are like my family and they have supported me. I have no interest in going out of country, those who are doing transgender work [...] then do it in front of us [...] I am doing this for those khwaja siras who have nothing and no one.
>
> (Butt 2020)

Ashee launches a firm critique of NGO funding economies and their uneven distributions, in a context where many *toli khwaja sira*s lack class capital, education, and language to access their entitlements, and instead foregrounds her relationalities with *khwaja sira* people, and the *ilaka*, through her art. As we outlined in the introduction through Reddy, the recognition of community rights to existence without providing mechanisms to redistribute power merely expands the reach of the state, forcing minority communities to reinscribe their marginality to claim entitlements, reifying pre-existing hierarchies of status and authenticity in the process (Reddy 2018: 55).

These *khwaja sira* performers reorient such hierarchies, and models of "useful citizenship" that evacuate performance. Building upon their long-cultivated affective networks of *vadhai*, many continue to perform, while also offering an alternative developmental model to top-down NGO projects. They translate rights paradigms to *khwaja sira* livelihood, shelter, and community entanglements across classes, religions, genders, sexualities, and kinships—and in the process expand their *deras*' relations in and beyond their *ilakas*, despite the increased contestations over these assemblages.

Futures

During my conversations and collaborations with various *toli* ensembles in September 2019, an article appeared in an English-language newspaper heralding the progress of Pakistan's transgender rights, that included a description of *vadhai*: "it *used to* be a regular tradition all across the sub-continent at the birth of a child where Khwaja Saras *used to* celebrate by dancing to welcome the newborn. People *used to* reward them in cash or kind that *used to* be the main source of their livelihood" (my emphasis, bin Ahsen 2019). In contrast to such a backward erasure—that speaks to the blindspots of class and neoliberal "progress"—I have shown that *vadhai* continues to move in and through these and other shifting orientations, across multiple bodies, spaces, feelings, scales, and temporalities. Beyond my particular focus in (mostly) Punjabi urban *ilakas* and in national forums, *vadhai* signals an abundance of other spaces, temporalities and repertoires for scholars to feel their way through. The persistence of *vadhai*'s repertoires, nurtured through *deras* and their lineages—while increasingly contested— put into play for many affective worldmaking, reorienting toward ever evolving attachments, proximities, and feeling elsewheres, as performers weave through, spin out, and make loose ends of multiscalar marginalizations. As such, performers retrace legacies of struggle, and survival, in performance over their lineages. One elder states that even under colonial criminalization in the Punjab, her *guru* "wouldn't do song and dance [...] or dress in women's clothes, but still vadhai went on," analogizing these struggles with her smuggling performance into anti-performance Wahabi houses today. Another proudly flaunts *ilaka* papers dating back to the nineteenth century and endorsed by the stamp of the colonial government. In a 2019 *gharoli roti*, celebrating her promotion in the lineage, she distributed gold rings embossed with the Empress of India's head to her *khwaja sira* family—that included her daughters in Amritsar, India. While visiting this extended family across the border, she shared a video of her being showered by buckets of *vail* in appreciation of her performance of a *lori*. Asserting futurity of her lineage, she bristles against the logics of colonial criminalization and contemporary nationalist borders. Another senior *guru* who began *vadhai* during the military regime of President Ayub Khan (r.1958–69), tells that when his government tried to ban *vadhai*, the *khwaja sira* Baba Faqiriya reminded Ayub Khan's mother that her *guru*s had held the President as a baby and sang him a *lori* (Kabutri 2019; Naqvi and Mujtaba 1997: 265). By making the Khans remember their relationships with her *khwaja sira guru*s, asserting emotional entanglements, the ban was quickly revoked. Indeed, just as the *hijrascape* survived the colonial period and periodic attempts at bans in postcolonial Pakistan, *vadhai* continues to weave in and out of bounded structures, rendering partial "territorializations" of these practices. Signaling precarity and perpetuity through the multiple affects *vadhai* generates, its performers continue to assert relationalities with each other and with their publics, and demand for more expansive feelings, opening paths to multiple futures.

3

Movements through *Badhai* Sonic Arrangements in India

Jeff Roy

One summer day in 2011, following a robust *suhoor* (meal eaten before dawn during Ramadan), Aiza-*guru* and I hop into her SUV to take a drive through the streets of Kanpur. She does not tell me where we are going or why we are going there. In fact, she does not say much at all, but blasts *qawwali* music with the windows rolled down, waving at passersby, many of whom appear to be familiar with the ritual. The sounds of honking rickshaws spill into the cabin of the vehicle and fold into the music, electrifying our cruise through the city. Turning onto a small road on the western edge of her *ilaka*, we find ourselves in an open field recently cleared for another cluster of apartments. Aiza parks the SUV behind a large dirt mound plopped at the end of a row of modest homes—some in mid-construction, typical of the area. A turn of the key cuts off the music in mid passage, and we cultivate a brief moment of tranquility. Our ears turn to the faint, rubbery sounds of a distant *dholak* that delicately ricochet off the concrete walls of the neighborhood, bouncing their way into the skeleton structures of half-built homes.

As we shuffle down a deserted *gali* (alley) following the source of the sound, the articulation of the drum coalesces into a syncopated *Keherwa taal*, an eight-beat rhythmic cycle commonly used in *qawwali*s and *bhajan*s. A *chaiwalla*'s call from afar accents the *taal* as we round another corner to see a *toli* of four materialize in the doorway of a house, where a group of small children are congregated. On approach, the music disintegrates, and Aiza is greeted by one of her *chela*s with a motion of the right hand to the feet. The *guru* embraces her and with the flick of her left wrist, signals the lead singer to launch into a *shadi* song in praise of the bridegroom for his material riches and other "natural" endowments. Listeners' ears perk up as the *badhai* begins to draw in the life of the neighborhood, turning unlocatability to locatibility, listening from afar to listening near.

Troubling fixed sensorial orientations and habits of writing informed by the colonial gaze, this chapter examines how *badhai* sonic arrangements are imbued with affective, sensorial, and political possibility (Kasmani 2017; Voegelin 2018). Layered with meaning for the communities in which they are heard, *badhai* sounds are always already interacting with a variety of place-specific sonic forms, such as the calls of street vendors, honking rickshaws, children's chitchatter, calls to prayer, metallic tinkerings of a kitchen, and other dissonant sounds from near and afar that may trigger or be triggered by the performances themselves. Like the fleeting and ephemeral interplay of Kasmani's sonic *mise-en-scène*—or "the heterogeneously constituted, always unfolding possibility of arrangement"—of Sufi shrines in Sehwan, Pakistan, *badhai*s are always "inflected in liaison with other sonic inputs," affective yet also intervene-able and steered to the articulation of certain feelings in sometimes dramatically different ways depending on the particular contexts to which they respond (Kasmani 2017). Beyond the signification of their lyrics, gestures, or what is heard within the range of normative hearing, *badhai* sounds also interact with unheard sonicities, echoes, whispers, smells, tastes, residual thoughts, ideas, beliefs, and other place-based significations that may be felt through a kind of acoustic haunting. They respond to and—through various forms of disruption—challenge the sensorial, social, cultural, and moral hierarchies of the neighborhood that otherwise "segregate, exclude and discriminate" their presences (Chandola 2010: 4–5). In many cases, *badhai* sonic arrangements even generate a particular attunement to sounding out and listening *beyond*—beyond control, musical coherence, what is expected materially of people and place, phenotypical belonging and social difference, normative arrangements of place-making, and dominant national imaginaries—bringing all those who inhabit a place towards new sonically-inflected sensorial possibilities. While the majority of scholarship on *trans-hijra* performance and performative embodiments centers visual utterances, listening and feeling through sound—as it interacts with other sensorial inputs—is nevertheless critical to understanding the relational, affective, and political dynamics of *badhai* and other cultural productions. This chapter traces the many possibilities generated by momentary interactions between *badhai* performers and listeners—all listeners, including the transient passersby—and the arrangements of the sounds and other senses produced by and folded into performance.

Politic(al Possibilitie)s of *Badhai* Sonic Arrangements

By politics of sound, I do not wish to specifically reference the roles that *badhai* or other transregional practices play in the changing economies of *trans-hijra* performance, nor do I seek to reference the roles of such performances in the formation of state policy or to mobilize voting blocs, or definitions of transgender for the purposes of bill formation—although this is indeed happening in *trans-hijra* circles, particularly in India's metropolitan areas, as I have witnessed and discussed elsewhere (Roy 2015a; 2016). Rather, I examine the practices and values that constitute "the activities of ordinary citizens who, through the exercise of their agency in contexts of public interaction, shape the conditions of their collective existence" (Hirschkind 2006: 8). As Tripta Chandola writes in reference to the sonic landscapes of Delhi's Govindpuri neighborhood, people's "engagements and experiences of sounds are socially, culturally, and morally informed and motivated and, thus, are essentially political in nature" (2011: 391–2). The experience of sounds, specifically as noise, is relational, significant to defining a sense of belonging, and tied to negotiations of space and community. Moreover, interactions with sound—humanly organized (music) or not—demand particular navigations and legislations, which may broadly impact the social, cultural, and political makeup of the urban landscape.

Badhai performances are always sites of contestation. Their sonic arrangements carry transregional histories of resistance that constitute places of intersubjective knowing, collective reflexivity, and action understood as necessary for engaging with, critiquing, and sometimes challenging normative codes of social and cultural engagement. "Arrangement" does not mean fixity, but "drift for composition and modulation," variation, and even disruption (Kasmani 2017; see Slaby et al.'s concept of "affective arrangement" [2019]). Folded into the sonic landscape of the neighborhood, *badhai* sonic arrangements lead to a thinking, feeling, and doing that push beyond conventional makings of place, with resonances that span localities and cross boundaries, including the moral parameters that undergird normative understandings of space, time, community, city, state, and nation. Queer and *trans-hijra* relationalities may become "the pathway to disorienting and palimpsestic landscapes [which] speak to the proximity of apparently disparate histories and geographic locations" (Gopinath 2018: 87), giving way to the possibility of a "queer regional imaginary" that stands in contradistinction to dominant national imaginaries that efface nonconforming bodies, desires, and affiliations (Gopinath 2018: 5). *Badhai*'s sonic arrangements emerge from and shape similar pathways across the *hijrascape*, carrying meaning that is tied to their movements and intersections, bearing possibilities of social and cultural resurgence across the places they touch through sound.

Notes on Sincerely Queer Listening

An exploration of *badhai* sonic arrangements necessitates a practice of listening that is flexible, relational, and resistant to settler colonial acts of listening which demand "fixed sensorial orientations" (Robinson 2020). This involves addressing the particular filters of race, class, caste, gender, sexuality, religion, and ability "that actively select and frame the moment of contact between listening body and listened-to sound" (Robinson 2020: 11), as well as de-composing a writing process that demands the rendering of sounds as objects distinct from other sensorial orientations, with content that is meant to be "found and rescued," consumed, and measured in relation to their analytic value—musical, social, or otherwise (Robinson 2020: 15).[1] While being mindful of connections to lands, cultures, traditions, and futurities that emerge from resurgent knowledges to which outsiders have limited embodied access, I draw from my own sensorial deviations across transcultural "queer collective memories" and kinship (Alexander 2006; Bakshi 2020; Khubchandani 2020; Prasad 2020b) through a sincere practice of queer listening.[2]

In July 2011, my relationship with Aiza is new, manifested through a queer network of friends in the Mumbai and Lucknow areas, where I had been living. Following on the heels of a trip to Bangkok, where a friend from Madurai underwent gender confirmation surgery (as shown in the documentary *Rites of Passage/Mohammed to Maya* [2011–12]), I find myself meandering with video and sound equipment in hand in the development of a film on *badhai*, later titled *Invisible Goddesses* (2011). My journeys lead to the streets or the dance floor, in the wings of a theater or in the front row of an audience, laboring in the capturing, editing, and release of performance video while cultivating intimacies with my sisters. Through this work, the bonds of *trans-hijra* belonging activate; I become someone's figurative "foreign *chela*" and her daughters' "*gora guru-bhai*" (brother or sister of the same *guru*, who is white), playing the stereotypically cinematic role both in front of and behind the camera as a uniquely, opportunely foreign *photo chela* with *chittiyaan kalaiyaan* ("white wrists"; Roy 2019a: 168–9). Our shared trust and willingness to explore intimacies, humor, and its proximate emotions inform our efforts to "reclaim the vulnerable ethnographic body," and all its contingent particularity, to open up spaces for critique (Jackson 2010: 279). Traversing different timezones, places, and cultures, we engage a politics of listening that accounts for the ways music and sound can be felt and sensed through our collaborative work, while confronting the hierarchies of authority and authenticity that continue to frame our transnational academic praxis.

Sincerely queer listening is sensual listening. It glides through and across multiple sensorial orientations, flexibly exploring the ways agency, experience, and perception of sound and music are collective and relational. It de-composes the rhythms and rhymes of fixed listening, however imperfectly, disobeying "preoccupations of authenticity by listening against [...] dominant discourses" (Balance 2016: 4–5). Writing *badhai* through sincerely queer listening is a drifting involved in, what Kasmani calls, "the cruising in queer zones of inter-subjective knowing that open up during fieldwork or become available in its wake through wispy registers of memory and intimacy" (2021c: 163). Its movements breathe through/give breath to the interstitial gaps in knowledge between seemingly fixed sensorial orientations, turning sensorial disorientations to reorientations, or lingering in disorientation, giving voice to that which evinces the "something beyond control" (Robinson 2020: 16), through adaptation, disruption, resurgence, and/or renewal. In the following sections, I explore these possibilities through "movements of narration" guided by audio and film footage, in order to illuminate the fleeting and ephemeral interplay of sound with other senses, and how certain scenes of heard and unheard sonic production are "continually inflected by the message and incremental character of atmospheres within which they arise and come to pass" (Kasmani 2017).[3] In doing so, I keep distance from the tendency to "straighten out" or "make whole" experiences of music and sound through feckless thick description and universalizing abstraction, to impart the sensibilities and affects of my "thin, cruisy, queer" writings with an emphasis on their fragmentations, frictions, fictions, and failures (2021c: 167).[4] Cruising between times and places informed by over a decade of memories, using film footage and notes as aids while also cognizant of the gaps such documentations magnify, the movements in this text resist linear temporality and spatial fixity, oscillating in resonance with the way the senses lead to certain feelings, how feelings lead to thoughts, thoughts lead to other thoughts and feelings, and so on. Delving into moments of deeper reflection and thought, the text lingers closeup in some areas, cultivating intimacy in the details. In other moments, perhaps somewhat unexpectedly, it zooms out and thrusts forward, jerks backward, or slips around temporalities and places, finding joy in movement. To accompany the writing, I offer a series of experiential short films, images, and audio recordings facilitating the activation and movement of the senses.[5]

Badhai Cruisings

A momentary pan of the camera and microphone orients the remote listener's senses to the low, dim sound of shuffling feet on patted, dry earth, punctuated by the nasalic call of the traveling *chaiwalla*. Standing outside the performance circle alongside my friend and situational assistant, a self-identified *kothi* from Kanpur, I have a camera to my face. Aiza and her *chela*s render us a couple, with me as the *panthi* (taking the dominant role), while I affirm reliable disloyalty to normative social scripts that write sexuality. "Double-decker," they whisper, chuckling while inferring sexual versatility. In the background, touching the top boundary of the visual frame, a father and his young daughter order a cold drink from a small stand. Loud chatter from the street fills the air as Aiza steps in to prepare her ensemble and their patrons—a Hindu family whose son recently married. Standing at the threshold with eyes and ears pointed towards Aiza, they appear to be ready for their *badhai*. (For the *toli*, *shadi badhai*s generally occur more frequently than *baccha* [child] or *makaan* [house] *badhai*s.)

Haree Sariwalli leads into the musical number with sharp, angular vocals in mixed Hindi and Bhojpuri-inflected dialect. Cutting to a closeup of the *dholak* player, the camera (my attention) gently pans upward to capture both musicians facing Aiza, who stands to their left, in the middle of the performance circle. Following a silent cycle into the song's *Keherwa taal*, the *dholak* begins its accompaniment of the vocal line with the aid of the *manjeera* played by Haree Sariwalli as she sings. Two supporting vocal parts enter the sonic arrangement as the song's call-and-response asks of them. The *sthai* (the song's primary theme or refrain, sung in the *madhya saptak*, or middle register) repeats while Aiza claps the *tal* with fingers splayed and palms firm. After a few beats, she lowers her hands to the *dholak* as a sign of respect, asking for *aashirwaad* (blessings) before finding her singing voice.

> Oh bridegroom, there is a precious ring in your hands
> (repeat)
> In your hands, there is a gardener's mori worth lakhs
> (repeat)
> Oh bridegroom, there is a precious ring in your hands
> (repeat)
> In your hands, there is a bracelet made of precious stones
> worth lakhs (repeat)
> Oh bridegroom, there is a precious ring in your hands
> (repeat) ...

The soft metallic kink of the *ghungroo* folds into the arrangement, crinkling in step with the *dholak* to tease the ear. Their generative sounds rebound around the concrete-lined *gali* like multicolored rubber balls, returning with a slight delay. (The balls travel far, reaching the ears of several neighbors one hundred yards down, who in mid conversation, begin to shamble their way in our direction.) The *badhai* is slowly surging through the life of the neighborhood, interacting with all the sounds that get produced by and/or folded into the performance. Momentary disorientations are leading to reorientations, transforming a landscape of indifference or fear into curiosity.

The sounds of queer chatter and laughter enter the sonic arrangement as Aiza plays to the camera during an articulated slow spin. With the briefest of smiles in my direction, she picks up the energy. Children's noise intensifies as a woman quietly approaches Aiza in mid gesture, whispering into her dancing ear to preview the destination of their next performance—a Muslim family who recently had a baby (as I find out later). The instrumentalists continue while Aiza stops briefly to exchange a few words before resuming her performance. My attention pans to the right to capture the trajectory of a passing motorcycle across the performance space. The vehicle parks to the left of the house as the music decays into quiet conversation. The audience of children behind me sit quietly wondering, while Aiza turns to the patron Auntie to scan her face for an emotional response.

Having piqued our collective interest, the performance quietly moves through the threshold of the home. The patrons are smiling at Aiza who, glowing in her white garments, positions herself in front of the *dholak* player seated against the wall inside the dimly lit foyer. Haree Sariwalli and her sister play-fight while flirting with the camera, giggling, just before the beginning of the next song. Clapping once to signal the musicians, Aiza crouches next to the *dholak* player as atmospheric chatter creates an echo chamber within the immediate vicinity of the home. Cutting through the noise, Haree Sariwalli's sharp voice leads into the *sthai* of the second song.

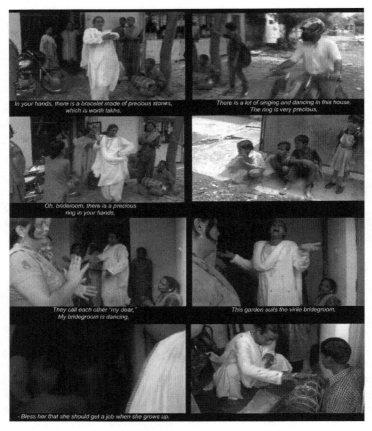

FIGURE 9 *Aiza*-guru *claps to* Keherwa taal *while dancing in the center of her* toli *as they perform at the threshold of a Hindu family's home. Children listen, amidst various neighborhood activities, whose sounds inflect and are infected by performance. Stills from the film* Invisible Goddesses *(Roy 2011).*

In Kasmani's sonic *mise-en-scène,* the delimited yet variable shapes forming the *what* of musical lyrical content poetically interact with the *where* of the performances, to create a "generative affectivity of sonic-scenes, a charged sense of time and place, feeling and mood that creates a dialogical relationship of believers' 'here' with an 'elsewhere'" (Kasmani 2017, bringing Amira Mittermaier's notion of "elsewhere" into dialogue with his "sonic scenes" [2011]). Communication with the elsewhere invites speculation, bringing possibility into practice as it signals the unseen, more-than-felt, sparsely registered dimensions of performance. *Badhai*'s communication with the elsewhere is not usually transcendental, in the sense that it leads to *sultana,* a moment of ecstasy, trance, or possession (Racy 2004). Rather, such communication is part of the contingent potential of the encounter, the "temporal realization dependent not only on the thing and what it holds before our encounter, but also on the context that frames the confrontation and enables the actions that are its possibilities produced in a creative reciprocal perception" (Voegelin 2018: 2). Salomé Voegelin likens these possibilities to momentary actions of light that produce a rainbow in the water bath, "whose colorful arch invites one to reconsider their understanding of light, water, and scientific knowledge" (Voegelin 2018: 3). *Badhai* invites listeners to contemplate their assemblage of bodies and instruments as arrangements that sonically combine to create what is possible in time and place.

Following her lead in, Haree Sariwalli moves the tempo, electrifying the place with the aid of the *manjeera* and *dholak.*

My bridegroom is a rich man / My bride is a rich woman
They call each other "my dear" / My bridegroom is
    dancing (repeat)
This garden suits the virile bridegroom (repeat)
He says "my dear" mischievously / My bridegroom is
    dancing (repeat)
My bridegroom is a rich man / My bride is a rich
    woman ...

With each variegated verse, the lyrics' capacity to invoke possibilities of a bountiful and fertile future invites a shift in affect. The use of the present tense in describing such possibilities—including the promise of wealth and possessions, expressions of marriage and heternormative love, dancing, and happiness—brings the future within reach, adding affective potency to the *badhai*. Aiza's luminescent dancing gestures to such imagined significations, transforming the place and those inhabiting/making it.

The call-and-response of the singers creates other important elements of arrangement. The repetition of the primary refrain by the lead singer, followed in unison by the supporting singers' responses, continues for eight cycles with gradually rising intensity. Accented undulations driven by the rhythm of the *dholak* chip away at the boundaries separating performers and listeners, performance and life. The more they call each other "my dear," the more they dance, the more possibilities of material abundance manifest through collective action, the more the *badhai* longs to de-compose normative makings of space to shape a *jagah* of creative abundance. Kasmani, et al., borrows Voegelin's notion of "interbeing" to enable affect's relational poignancy and capacity for resisting partitionings of time, space, and bodies through the experience of being "in-between" and "with-each-other" (2020: 92). Reciprocal interbeing makes thinkable that which may not be, at least under usual circumstances, shaping how we experience "more fully the here" in elsew*here* (Kasmani et al. 2019; 2020: 93) through the "plural participation" of performers and listeners in the shared production of a possible situation (Voegelin 2018: 43). Through this process, it "reminds us of our responsibility in the interpretation and valuation of that circumstance: our ethical position and positioning as communicating agents in an interrelated sphere" (Voegelin 2018: 48). Our plural participation in this rippling sonic arrangement enables and is enabled by the facilitation of *izzat*, a moral positioning of respect which shapes relationalities between *guru*s and their *chela*s, sisters and their sisters and lovers, performers and other sincerely queer listeners.

It enables us to feel the *here* in elsewhere, an atmosphere in which vocality and instrumentality, their generative potentialities, and the artistic and spiritual experiences of all performers and listeners are realized through intimate reciprocal interbeing.[6]

Haree Sariwalli, Aiza, and her *chela*s do not bother to sing in *sur* (precise intonation), and no one seems to mind. Rubbing up against musical coherence gives way to possibilities of humor and pleasure as sonic frictions slip into and shape the texture of this place. Aiza periodically sings in the direction of her *chela*s, using *abhinaya* to carry this potential, playfully inviting us in while drawing from established histories and musical practices that inform *badhai* pedagogies throughout South Asia.[7] The quality of her voice and orientation of her gaze create other layers of intimacy. At times, it feels like she is gesturing to us individually, summoning us to participate (perhaps as her *chela*), teasing us to respond (perhaps as her lover). The patrons are animated by this performance, reacting in some cases by clapping, tapping the feet, or lightly bouncing up and down on the heels. With a couple of thrusts of the hip from one side to the next, I join in the merriment, signaling anxiety in my awkward "gay *gora*" way.

In *badhai*s throughout many parts of India, voices are conceptualized as gifts from the Mother Goddess, or conduits through which the goddesses Murga or Bahuchara Mata are able to communicate and bestow their blessings, invoking religious legitimacy (Roy 2015a: 198). In some *badhai*s—especially in contexts of pronounced religious or spiritual devotion on the part of Hindu-identified performers and listeners—the stated or implicit invocation of the Mother Goddess manifested through lyrical content and singers' voices serves to personify the possibility of connection with an otherworldly elsewhere. I recall a personalized demonstration from Arya and her *chela*—organized by the Gujarati Prince Manvendra Singh Gohil in Surat, Gujarat—of the *badhai* song "Asha Natoru". Grabbing hold of two metallic water cups to use as rhythmic accompaniment in place of a *dholak*, Arya leans into the song in perfect *sur*. In the final *tihai* (three-part rhythmic refrain),

the singers call on the presence of the Goddess to appear in the
room and bless the audience through their voices:

Ao mai re bhala tum jago mai re
Mileko bako mai re
Jisi ki lodh lagavi re
Gale mein aj samao re!
(Please come with all your glory,
Oh Goddess I'm yearning to meet you,
That's all I want,
Through my throat/voice you sing!) (Roy 2017: 409; see
    Roy 2015a: 198)

While the Goddess is not directly invoked in this manner, Aiza's
badhai creates the possibility for a similar kind of dialogue.
The particular conditions of performance, and the way the
utterance of words interact with other place-based sounds and
sonicities within the context of the home's foyer, orient listeners
and doers towards the belief in the possibility of blessings
coming true. Nevertheless, it is the invisible embrace of sounds
themselves and their sonic arrangement that make the difference
in this situation. These sounds are imperfect, beautiful, and
their particular variations, disruptions, and interactions with
melodious and dissonant sounds alike, compel listeners and
performers to feel, imagine, and/or act in different ways.

Several layers of intentionally-produced sounds are imbued
with the special power of affecting any number of emotional
possibilities. The *manjeera* in the higher register, the *dholak* in
the lower, the *ghungroo* and clapping in the middle, all hold
special status for their abilities to articulate rhythm and interact
with the sonic texture of the space differently. As demonstrated
in the opening vignette of this text, these sounds combine to
form an interlaced, rhythmic trellis upon which the melody,
carried by the voice, grows. With them comes a sensation
of being lifted. At the same time, the *dholak*'s syncopated
Keherwa taal anchors the rhythm for the dance, lower body
hip thrusts, gestures, *abhinaya*, and other embodied forms

of communication to respond. Dancing also facilitates the sonic pull of the drum, forming a nucleus of social activity around its immediate vicinity. The drum's timbre, undulating pitch, and sheer volume serve as a sonic beacon for those afar, outside of the visual range of the *badhai* performance, while they tug at the feet, legs, hips, core, chest, arms, and head for those in close proximity. As the *dholak* pulls the abdomen into the source of the sound, clapping provides a direction for the head to turn.

These expressions of sonic difference continue to interact dramatically with the noises of the neighbourhood within and immediately surrounding the home, as they combine with sonic inputs from *badhai* instruments, chatter, laughter, calls from the *chaiwalla*, rickshaw honks, and/or dissonant sounds from near or afar. Chandola writes about how the sensorial ordering of certain sounds in urban landscapes are articulated through the act of "listening into others," a process used to segregate, exclude, and discriminate against the presences of unwanted sounds and affects (2010: 4–5). *Badhai*'s generative sonic arrangements and their ability to signal recognizable difference challenge the already open and discerning ear of what it thinks it already knows. They also have the capacity to reorient listeners differently, depending on what other sorts of sounds are being produced both near and far, turning the unfamiliar, strange, or absurd, into something known, felt, possible. This lies not only in *badhai*'s capacity to disseminate ideas or instill religious ideologies through lyrics, clothing, or other non-sonic significations, "but in its effect on the human sensorium, on the affects, sensibilities, and perceptual habits of its [...] audience" (Hirschkind 2006: 2). In this case, "the soundscape produced through [and interacting with] the circulation of this medium animates and sustains the substrate of sensory knowledges and embodied aptitudes undergirding" the urban landscape (Hirschkind 2006: 2). *Badhai*'s sonic arrangements find their ways into and disrupt normative soundscapes to create sensorial knowledges that allow for other affective possibilities with others, within and outside of their immediate community. Their disruptions are invitational, leading to pleasure, humor, and even irritation or aggravation, sometimes in the same performance.

The emotional direction of the sonic arrangement, the cultivation of interbeing in this moment, and the transformations they bring to the place, compel Auntie to request additional blessings on behalf of her younger daughter. In a possible challenge to the cisheteronormative order of the neighborhood, she asks, "Before you go, bless [my daughter] that she should get a job when she grows up." Aiza makes this happen without question or additional negotiation, having already received the patrons' modest offerings of money, rice, and flour. She blesses the *dholak* and gently ushers the *toli* to respectfully part the scene.

Possibilities of Recovery and Renewal

Badhai's movements are shaped not only by the arrangements of sounds produced by and folded into performance, but also through the pedagogical practices of the *dera*, which are informed by Aiza's love for music, her *gharana*'s oral history, and the *izzat* contouring relations with her eight *chela*s and *guru-nani*. Two weeks following our *badhai* outing, we feel our way through the tone of a wandering conversation, code-switching between Hindi-Urdu and English, sitting cross-legged on Aiza's bedroom floor in front of a sleeping *guru-nani* (whom Aiza later explains is unwell). Over *chai*, she summarizes her understanding of the *gharana*'s history for me:

> In Kanpur, the very first guru had two chelas, one Muslim and one Hindu. They created their own gharanas—the Miya is the Muslim gharana and Gangarami is the Hindu gharana. Gangarami also has Muslim chelas and gurus. Like them, we also have many Hindu chelas. We were Muslims for only four generations, but the guru before that was Hindu. Our gharana is actually as old as Akbar. We came from Agra and our songs come from there.

Aiza references India's history of religious cohabitation and the importance of keeping doors open. "My chelas come from Hindu, Muslim, and Christian families, and I accept them all. Though we are a Muslim gharana and I am Muslim, they do not have to fully convert [to Islam] and do namaz. They can also do puja," she says with muted pride and joy. "There is no Hindu-Muslim bullshit here, although there is outside of this circle," she says while tracing the boundaries of the floor with her index finger. "I don't care where my chelas come from, although I prefer to avoid scheduled caste," she concedes. Sensing a question, she clarifies that indeed "they can become my chelas, but it is more difficult since we cannot eat together." This points to the persistence of untouchability, caste hierarchies, and other practices that continue to impact *Dalit* (oppressed caste) and other communities throughout India. *Trans-hijra* and queer *Dalit* communities regularly feel the weight of caste in the largely upper caste/class-dominated LGBTQIA+ activist spaces through acts of exclusion, erasure, objectificaton, fetishization, and intimate forms of violence (Dutta 2018; Kang 2016a, 2016b). Though, indeed, caste may also find its way into the *dera* and other non-cisheteronormative, non-Hindu contexts. Changing the beat slightly, Aiza continues:

> Whatever my gurus and forefathers have been doing, that can never go out of my heart and mind, and I follow it […] When I choose a chela, the only thing I ask is that if they go around in the neighborhood, they should talk properly, nicely, and decently to everyone. They should listen to what I say and do household work. Similarly, a guru should talk to people properly and a guru should know how to differentiate what is good and what is bad, because that will pass on.

While Aiza demonstrates a particular devotion to her faith, she does not demand the same of her Muslim *chela*s. Only one participates fully in Ramadan, "since they have to wear lipstick and makeup to dance in badhais." Aiza clarifies, "they can actually go without lipstick to badhai, but they usually won't because if they don't it will look plain, and they have to dance and it won't add that 'zing.' Some of them have paan addictions as well." Chuckling, she explains that "there is a different namaz for a different time, and they practice all of them." (Aiza's *guru* usually practices Ramadan, although illness is preventing her from strict observance.) Turning towards me, Aiza shares that "when someone is not fasting but sitting next to someone who is fasting, they [receive] equal blessings." I thank her for her kindness and comment on the auspicious nature of our meeting. Aiza's embrace points both to the continuing legacy of pluralism that informs *hijra-khwaja sira* intersubjective knowing, speaking to a performance of inclusion that challenges normative codes of social and cultural engagement, albeit with some notable caste-based limitations.

Creating inclusive, flexible repertoire builds understanding and rapport with patrons. For Aiza and her *chela*s, this benefits both parties, often resulting in a larger share for the troupe, which can range anywhere from Rs. 500 to the tens of thousands. On the day of the *badhai* outing, decompressing after our cruises through the *ilaka*, Aiza and I sit on the floor of her bedroom as she quietly separates the ensemble's earnings of Rs. 6,000. Two thousand are divided among the three participating *chela*s and *dholak* player, then placed into separate bundles. The troupe's lead singer receives 800 while the others each receive 400. The remaining 4,000 goes to Aiza and *guru-nani*. (As Aiza later explains, these splits conform to how Muslim *gharana*s typically divide their earnings. Hindu *gharana*s, like Gangarami, divide their earnings in half, in which *guru*s receive 50 percent of the share, leaving the rest to performing *chela*s and instrumentalists [Roy 2015a: 187–8]).

While Aiza concentrates on the cash, the ensemble waits patiently at the door of the bedroom, caressing the space with bated breath. Having just emerged from a short nap, *guru-nani* quietly observes our interactions, slowly developing a look of curiosity on her face. Sensing *guru-nani*'s dawning gaze, Aiza switches on the television to a soap already in progress, then calls on her *chela*s to receive their shares. (Money for the *dholakwalla* is generally delivered by the head *chela*.) In order of rank, they take their turns strutting through the room, smiling self-consciously, as if auditioning for a role in a film. Glowing in mid-strut, Neelee Sariwalli offers to perform a *badhai* number. Aiza, with a subtle roll of the eyes, agrees and begins to prepare the *dholak*.

Haree Sariwalli positions herself on the floor with the *dholak* in the center of the room. On the downbeat of the *filmi* number "Laal Dupatta" ("Red Shawl"), the atmosphere of the small bedroom is jolted by layers of sounds as though a raw telephone wire had entered water. These sounds are focused, crisp, unambiguous, and unobstructed by sonic inputs that typically get triggered by and/or folded into *badhai* performance in public settings. The close confines of the cement-walled room intensify the colors of the *dholak*—light and monotone on the surface (warm with lighter value), yet also deep, round, resonant, and rich with overtones (cool with darker value). Although dancing is happening, the vocals lead the way through all their variations, combining in unexpected, dissonant ways to produce overtones typically heard through the production of perfect fifth intervals. The addition of Aiza's *manjeera* in the middle of the song adds a quixotic hue and lavish texture to the sonic arrangement. My attention pans to Aiza, who looks directly into the camera with inviting eyes and a slight smirk on her face. She winks, then joins in song as a look of intensity washes over her face. My attention pans back to the center of the room to see *guru-nani* now sitting on the edge of the bed at full attention, with shoulders hunched to the edges of a big smile.

The performance eventually disintegrates and I ask for a *jaccha baccha* song. The lead singer begins with a short introduction, followed by a burst of energy from the *dholak* and supporting singer's introductory *sthai*: "Lag Na Jaye Nazariya" ("May No One Cast an Evil Eye") (Earlier that day, I hear the ensemble perform this song for a Muslim family, though clear listening is obstructed by sounds from the street.) This song is swifter in tempo, lighter yet more focused in its emotional direction. The intimate cultivation of reciprocal interbeing in this moment compels *guru-nani* to jump spontaneously from her seat and dance. Twirling around with arms in the air, she lip-syncs to the lyrics, communicating joy through *abhinaya*. We are all transported. In this time and place, the sonic arrangement pulls inward, resonating with the memories, histories, and intimacies of the *dera* to facilitate recuperative acts of another kind. It gives way to the formation of "other bodily orientations" and enables that which is otherwise inaccessible (LaBelle 2021: 82), providing the taste of transformation and a possibility of recovery and renewal.

Im/Possibilities

Following the performance, our conversation meanders in a slightly different direction, as I wonder what possibilities *badhai* sonic arrangements may bring to locations elsewhere, outside the *dera*, *ilaka*, and Kanpur itself. Our discussion finds its way to New Delhi, where India's HIV/AIDS NGOs are organizing for the introduction of transgender rights bills. Aiza explains that she considers her *gharana*'s positioning within the context of contemporary *trans-hijra* rights as somewhat independent from that of the largely Hindu-dominant, English-speaking elite dominating political discourse on prominent nationwide network news channels. Although she is aware of such efforts by the NGOs and public figures, she and her *chela*s are "sorted," unbothered with respect to daily life, business, or identity for her to care about moving into such circles of ascendancy and power. While Aiza appears undaunted, sincerely queer listening amplifies the sound of concern in her voice, translating a display of quiet indifference into something even more meaningful.

My memories fast forward four years to a moment in which the staging of *badhai* song and other performances at the 3rd National *Hijra Habba* (festival, in Kannada) produce multiple, sometimes conflicting affective, sensorial, and political possibilities. In July 2015, I am invited to assist the India HIV/AIDS Alliance in filming the event, and with their collaboration, shoot and edit a short promotional film entitled *India's Big Push for Transgender and Hijra Welfare* (Roy 2015c).

Performing with some of India's celebrity activists and political leaders in the front rows of the audience—including the Minister of Social Justice and Empowerment, Shri Thaawar Chand Gehlot—NGO members and affiliates speak to the government's commitment to the "ongoing struggle for rights, respect, and dignity for the transgender community in India and […] around the world" (Roy 2015c). Highlighting the *Pehchan* (identity) Program—"implemented by India HIV/AIDS Alliance and partners across 18 Indian states to build the capacity of community-based organizations and to enhance the HIV response for vulnerable and underserved MSM, transgenders and hijras"—leaders express interest in taking "this movement forward to create change and build our identity." Tripathi is one of the speakers present, often taking to the podium to rally our bodies in all their disparate assemblages.

Towards the beginning of the program, a short performance featuring a *badhai* practitioner serves as an "arrival call" for the *habba*'s staged functions—a possible nod to the community's "rich cultural tradition" that formed part of the argument paving the way for transgender rights legislation (Roy 2016: 416). However, just as the singer is able to reach a moment of emotional release, the performance is seemingly interrupted and the practitioner is led off the stage. (This footage is not included in the film.) Later in the program, Tripathi delivers a speech adding additional meaning to these actions:

> We can do some badhai so we can earn 11,000, or 1,500, or 500 rupees to survive for one day. If we keep thinking like this, then we will be begging for another 200 years, and our future generations will be selling their bodies for 20 and 50 rupees each.
>
> (Roy 2015c)

The speech continues to emphasize the importance of cultivating skills through mainstream professions, making "use of the policies *they* bring forth" for personal empowerment alongside the suggestion of *badhai*'s renunciation. Upon the speech's conclusion, the front rows of the audience erupt into applause, while the *trans-hijra* community members sitting in the back signal silent resistance. Indeed, the speech seeks a conciliatory tone in the presence of India's NGO and political elite, reproducing overgeneralized representations of *trans-hijra* livelihood—including *badhai*'s conflation with begging— that lend credence to bankroll the "singular narrative of transgender individuals performing nationalism to seek citizenship rights" (Bhattacharya 2019: 19). Such actions complicate, suppress, and stifle the diversity of experiences and expressions—particularly those that elude the logics of neoliberal and religious nation-building—represented in the back of the room. (Earlier that year, Tripathi shared with me her intention to run for local office in the state of Maharashtra, yet her leanings towards the Hindu Right were only just being made known, and the remarks she delivered expressing anti-Pakistan sentiments had yet to air (Upadhyay 2020). Nevertheless, it is around this time that Tripathi began participating in the formation of the Akhil Bharatiya Kinnar Akhada, signaling movement away from the community's religious and spiritual polyvocality).

In Pakistan, Kasmani points to the ways transgender and *khwaja sira* collective organization untethers individuals from difficult histories to offer new means of future making (2021a). Facilitated by individuals and organizations in power, this work opens some doors while foreclosing other already-present affective, sensorial, and political possibilities of being and belonging. While *badhai*'s staging at the *habba* offers opportunities for practitioners to celebrate their collective negotiations with certain cultural histories and practices, its unique treatment as an abject other or spoiled commodity reinforces fixed standards and moral parameters to *badhai*'s reception that do little but repeat "the rhythms of colonization" (Spivak 1993: 53). The speech delivered by Tripathi, the limited time allotted to the practitioner, and the absence of critical discussion addressing the structural inequities that have contributed to the subjugation of such performances and practitioners (Reddy 2018) all render *badhai* as visible, but not *heard* or felt. Gopinath points to how "imperial, settler colonial, and racial regimes of power work through spatial practices that order bodies and landscapes in precise ways [and] instantiate regimes of vision that determine what we see, how we see, and how we are seen" (2018: 7). Such sensorial constrictions centering fixed visibility as a precondition to inclusion, social reform, and wellbeing within the context of the *habba*, risks "at risking" or asterisking (Tuck and Yang 2012) the diverse voices of *badhai* practices and practitioners in the room. These constrictions carry the residues of colonial denigration facilitating the visual regime, while exacerbating exploitations of caste, class, and religious privileges across the country which continue to push non-dominant individuals, *dera*s, and *gharana*s "off stage," further into the peripheries of power and influence (Upadhyay 2020).

Alongside *badhai*'s othering, the *habba*'s staging of professional performances further attests to the lingering presence of the colonial visual regime working to erase any "shadow of doubt or ambiguity" (Arondekar 2009: 88) in the representation of certain performing bodies as exemplary national subjects. Such performances evince the importance of "being seen but not heard," reproducing sensorial hierarchies that slip towards tenuous affective and political possibilities. The performances are arranged and choreographed by the Dancing Queens, whom I have worked with before, and include a series of numbers set to recorded music staggered intermittently throughout the day, each showcasing the troupe's abilities and talent. Among the numbers are included an interpretive performance by the troupe's leader and her birth mother indexing their journey through various transformations in their relations. The main character's experience of joining a *hijra gharana* serves as the central conflict in the narrative, as she is found begging in the streets, falling victim to sexual violence, and eventually returning to her birth mother whose initial resistance eventually gives way to loving acceptance. This leaves spectators ruminating on the bittersweetness of their reunion against the backdrop of a particularly bleak vision of *hijra* culture. I have seen a rendition of this performance elsewhere (Roy 2015d; Roy 2019a: 179–80), and similar narratives detailing the gaps of affection between children and their natal family (particularly mothers) appear in my interviews with other performers, in popular films, news features, and texts (see Khubchandani's story of Ehmad, 2020: 151–2). If, as Ahmed suggests, the familiar is "the world we implicitly know as a world that is organized in specific ways" (2006: 124), the performance draws on the viewer's familiarity with fractured familial narratives to produce relatively predictable affective arrangements.

As we explore in the book's introduction, acoustic recycling of *filmi* music in *badhai* shapes the contact between bodies through shared knowledges and histories, drawing from popular repertoires and/or those with queer significations. In my ambulations across *badhai* sonic arrangements throughout parts of Gujarat, Maharashtra, and Uttar Pradesh, known classics like "Saj Gai Gali" ("The Street is Decorated") and "Bano Teri Akhiyaan Surmi Daani" ("Oh Bride, Your Eyes Are Lined with Kajal") often emerge as they may be heard queerly by listeners while imparting sentiments about the birth of a baby or marriage, respectively (Roy 2015a: 20–1). The *habba*'s staged performances, however, carry a different social and political utility. In their curation of familiar narratives and routines, the performances organize the dissemination and mainstreaming of certain ideas and political ideologies by working to make the strange common, the distant proximate, the impossible possible. In doing so, the detachment of what is seen (dance/movement/lip-syncing) from what is heard, coupled with the physical distance and height of the stage

FIGURE 10 *Abheen Aher (center) and the Dancing Queens perform at the 3rd National* Hijra *Habba in New Delhi, India. Still from the film* India's Big Push for Transgender and Hijra Welfare *(Roy 2015c).*

(limiting touch, smell, taste, and to an extent, sight), constrict the senses and compel viewers to yield to the primacy of the visual regime.

Eventually, the audience reaches its limit of ocular intake. A sense of impatience sweeps over the space, achieving a level that the boundaries of the stage cannot control. Towards the middle of another number, members of the audience, facilitated by Tripathi, lance themselves onto the stage to dance in small groups, disrupting the Dancing Queens' carefully planned and skillfully performed choreography. A mix of smiles accent the collisions between laughter and recorded music, vexing and dissonant yet beautiful. The seated audience members seem unsure of how to feel, whether or not to intervene, how to participate. This is the kind of failure found on the queer dance floor, a kind of art that transforms the rhythms and rhymes of place into something else altogether, pushing what is shown on stage into the wings, shifting absences into excesses, turning impossibilities into possibilities.[8] The oscillation between shock and awe, among other things, feels fitting of "the fact that sometimes riding the razor's edge between our perverse existence and the perversions of modern institutions [like our political institutions] is part of the fun" (Ochoa 2014: 15; in Khubchandani 2020: 7).

Dissonance, Disorientation, and Negation

With every *badhai* performance comes different, sometimes conflicting affective, sensorial, and political possibilities. In this movement, I recall through my experiences with Juneeta Singh-*guru* how *badhai* performances can sometimes delve into more dissonant realms, in which the potential for conflict leads to openings of disaccord and friction between all parties involved. Cruising through my memories and previous sketches (see Roy 2015a), I consider the ways in which *badhai* sonic arrangements lead to differently disorienting affective possibilities for performers and listeners, where disorientation leads to the sensation of "being displaced and unplaceable in the alienating landscape of heteronormativity" (Gopinath 2018: 71). Instead of giving way to reorientation, in which the rhythms and rhymes of place are transformed to create parallel alterior emplacements of belonging, we are pulled into a space of "unknowing, and unlocatability" (Gopinath 2018).

By the time we meet, Juneeta is already in the process of negotiations to establish her own *gharana* in a developing area on the outskirts of Lucknow. At 26 years of age, Juneeta is optimistic about her ability to establish a reputable lineage. "I boycotted my guru [...] to become independent and to own my area," she tells me. Juneeta's former *gharana*'s name is Mevachati, although I am unsure about its status because it takes her a minute (with help from one of her *chela*s) to recall the name. The *ilaka* she seeks to claim is a mix of lower middle-class homes and empty lots (still in development, like Aiza's) encompassing about ten square kilometers in and surrounding a neighborhood called Jankipuram.

Weaving through the contested neighborhood, our colorful *toli* of six attracts the attention of neighborhood youths. Swooping in with big grins, two young men seize the harmonium and *dholak* that had begun to cramp our queerish gait. Forgoing the opportunity to fraternize with them, Juneeta coyly slips away from the scene to knock on the door of a modest shotgun-style home. An unexpectedly long exchange of words signals unambiguous resistance from the abode's tenants, but with the sound of a clap, Juneeta passes decisively through the threshold. Once inside, Juneeta makes her way towards an elderly widow sitting on a couch, whispers into her ear, and with a gentle tap on the top of her bald head, performs a blessing. Smiling while trembling, an Auntie pours chilled water into a glass and hands it to Juneeta.

Juneeta's floral-dressed *chela* steps in to lead the troupe through three songs, dancing to the groovy cross-rhythm carried by the *dholak* and metronomic clapping. The harmonium carries the melodies while she fudges the lyrics. Despite its obvious underlying frictions, the performance is well-received by the youthful roadies, whose numbers seem to multiply just outside the foyer threshold. Their eyes twinkle as the dancer twirls her *Salwar Kameez* (long tunic worn over trousers) to the jingle of her *ghungroo*. However, at the conclusion of the third song, Auntie presents a basket of offerings containing a less-than-adequate sum of *rupee*s. A conflict ensues as Juneeta pleads for more. Without skipping a beat, Auntie retorts: "You don't even belong here. You bring your kind somewhere else!" A heavy flurry of curses sweeps us out onto the street. Flushed and deflated, we scurry off with instruments and offerings in hand, Rs. 2,000 short of Juneeta's goal (Roy 2015a).

Back inside the car, I turn my attention to the fearless *guru*. She leans over to me as if wanting to rest on my shoulder, but instead straightens her back and turns the other way. Our conversation skirts around the subject of the fight, touching on the look and stature of the neighborhood boys. In the middle of some flighty banter, in which she shares what complications arise from sex, Juneeta's face turns green and she asks her driver to pull over. Opening the door, she leans out without moving an inch from her seat, takes care of business, and signals the driver to move on, returning to the conversation smiling, seemingly unfazed. Sincerely queer listening through the silence allows me to identify this moment as more than just a product of nausea, but a slightly delayed experience of negation.

Merleau-Ponty illustrates how moments of disorientation may involve the experience of disorder as well as "giddiness and nausea, which is the awareness of our contingency, and the horror with which it fills us" (2002: 296). But, as Ahmed shows, the sensation of losing orientation as the body becomes an object alongside others is one of nausea *and* negation, where "the crisis of losing one's place in the world [is] a loss of something that one has yet to be given" (2006: 139). "To feel negated is to feel pressure upon one's bodily surface, where the body feels the pressure point as a restriction in what it can do" (2006: 139), leading to momentary loss of the senses, restrictions in bodily mobility, incapacitation, and/or indeed, digestive instability. While disorientation "may be the source of vitality as well as giddiness [in which we] may find joy and excitement in the horror," in situations where bodies "are not extended by the skin of the social," such freedom of movement is not easy (Ahmed 2006: 4, 139). For Juneeta in this unfamiliar, hostile *ilaka*-to-be, the body is forced to take a different direction, becoming a site of social stress as movement through the senses is halted. In the time and place of the car, in which we may return to *hear* one another sincerely, we can feel the cisheteronormative sensorial, affective, and political order of the contested neighborhood remain intact, but not entirely unscathed.

Breaking Fast and Erotic Possibilities

In recovery from the experience of nausea, I return to an evening in which Aiza, my friend, and I share *iftar* (meal eaten after sunset during Ramadan) under the comforting glow of a candle. A plate of dates, *pakoras*, *mithai*, *bakhoor* incense, and the pungent sound of a distraught neighborhood child fills the space with sweet aroma. After Aiza performs *namaz* with one of her neighbors, she opens the door to a shrine located on the far end of her bedroom, lighting incense to conduct a few more prayers. The smell of old books and sandalwood emerges from the secret lair, and with it, a signal of trust. We sit down for more conversation over *chai*, chatting and cultivating intimacy around the subject of prayer and devotion. Eventually, the decision is made to visit the city *masjid*, and Aiza robes herself in a white-collared dress shirt and jeans.

Under the green glow of a mosque in the center of town, we make ourselves at home on a few plastic chairs situated in a semicircle behind a *dhaba* (roadside restaurant). Aiza leaves us briefly for *namaz*, and rejoins us moments later for food. The sounds of bicycle chimes, motorcycle horns, street vendors, and vintage bollywood music permeates the place, carrying with them the scent of *shami* and *galawati kebab*s, buffalo meat, smoke. My hands are shaking, creating an unstable camera frame, as the *dhabawalla* delivers *chai*. Aiza whips out a smartphone to play the *alap* (improvisatory prologue) to Abida Parveen's "Mast Qalandar" ("Ecstatic Qalandar" [a Sufi saint]) and on cue, another *dhabawalla* comes to receive our order while humming softly in *sur*. He seems to know Aiza well, perhaps even intimately, but keeps his signals subtle in front of an audience of three. Aiza gushes over him as she conveys our desire for sustenance. Blushing, he turns away to deliver the order. As his hums trail into the distance, Aiza claims the tune with slightly increased volume and fully formed lyrics:

Oh Jhulelal, always keep my honour,
Of Sindri, of Sehwan, my friend, Shabaaz Qalandar,
With every breath, I recite Qalandar, Ali is in my every
    breath,
With every breath, I recite Qalandar, Ali is number one.

The sight and sound of Aiza's singing attracts the attention of a few more friends from the increasingly busy market. One embraces Aiza and joins our threesome, adding his voice to the chorus. The sky is fully dark when the food arrives, and a rush of *kabob*, *keema*, *roti*, and rice fill our guts in minutes. We are becoming intoxicated.

My friend erupts spontaneously into song when one of Aiza's sisters dressed in male clothes comes to join us. Three more young men surround Aiza to shower her with attention. One of them asks if he can take a picture of our motley crew, while another challenges us to sing a *qawwali*. Feeling exposed by whiteness, I jump in with a hilariously *fireng* rendition of Abida Parveen's "Tere Ishq Nachaya" ("Your Love Made Me Dance"). When I inevitably stumble under the weight of the lyrics, the others jump in for the recovery. "Shabash, kya baat hai!" (colloquialisms for "Bravo!" or "Well done!") Our queering of place under the *masjid*'s incandescence, facilitated by our mediated song, interacts delicately with the echoes, whispers, thoughts, ideas, beliefs, and other place-based significations that linger over the course of the day through a kind of acoustic haunting. The residues of the day get folded into our sonic arrangements and, with the aid of other sensorial inputs—such as the smells, tastes, and feels of delicious food (and friends)— direct us to experience new possibilities. We are arranging a new kind of *badhai*, interacting with and transforming the rhythms and rhymes of our vicinity to create parallel alterior emplacements of belonging. These possibilities enter into the erotic, reorienting the senses of some transient passersby, challenging the neighborhood's sonic landscapes of indifference, leaning into pleasure. For other passersby, unable or unwilling to listen queerly, the sound of our gleeful performance simply folds into the din of the increasingly bustling sonic landscape of the neighborhood. We seem to inhabit multiple realities at the same time while oscillating between layers of sound and being, uncovering a sense of familiarity and comfort in the possibilities of all or none.

Moving through muddled negotiations of language, desire, and intimacy, my attention swings between Aiza and my friend, who seem tethered to each other through song. Gliding across the sounds of the words, we slip into the spaces between, entwining our bodies through shared exploration on the edge of ecstasy. Our sincerely queer listening takes on a generative dimension, activating new sensorial and affective possibilities, inhabiting the unmarked places of music-making and composition, giving voice to sound through embodied spaces of creative improvisation.

Listening Forward

Cruising across different sonic landscapes, this chapter addresses the sensorial, affective, and political possibilities of *badhai* sonic arrangements. Writing *badhai* through sincerely queer listening, I show how such arrangements respond to and, through various forms of disruption, transform the sensorial, social, cultural, and moral landscapes undergirding the cisheteronormative neighborhood that otherwise negates the bodies and cultural practices of *badhai* practitioners. In some cases, these sonic arrangements bring all those who inhabit a place towards new sonically-inflected sensorial possibilities, interacting with other sensorial inputs to rearrange the rhythms and rhymes of place to create parallel alterior emplacements of belonging. In other cases, they lead to differently disorientating affective possibilities, lingering in spaces of unknowing and unlocatability (Gopinath 2018: 71), nausea and negation (Ahmed 2006: 139). Placed in conversation with different staged sensorial, affective, and political im/possibilities at the *Hijra Habba*, I show how the reception of *badhai* and other performances are constricted and fixed sensorially, leading to controlled—yet not unchallenged—affective and political possibilities. Cruising under the luminescent *masjid*, I find myself listening forward to imagine what other possibilities may arise through *badhai*'s many sensorial, physical, technological, and conceptual arrangements. I continue to ruminate on the violence of colonial modernity in queer and *trans-hijra* spaces—*dera*s, *ilaka*s, streets, and *dhaba*s—through "the consigning of gendered, sexualized, and racial marked bodies to hypervisibility and/or invisibility within a hegemonic visual field" (Gopinath 2018: 170) and other means which foreclose other possibilities of being and belonging. I continue to wonder how writing *badhai* through sincerely queer listening—like Gopinath's queer visioning of the regional imaginary—may allow us to discover "the intertwined nature of the historical forces that produce this in/visibility [enabling] us to grasp the unanticipated intimacies between bodies, temporalities, and geographies" that are the product of overlapping histories of colonial modernity, postcolonial nationalism, racialization, and transnational migration (Gopinath 2018: 170). I imagine what such listening may do in the field to trouble habits of scholarly writings and other representations of queerness, *trans*ness, *hijra*-ness, and *khwaja sira*-ness in South Asia and elsewhere. I lean in to listen forward to the whispers and echoes that make of our own placements in all of this, informing us of how we might all be transformed in the process.

Further Notes on an Inconclusive Practice …

Adnan Hossain,
Claire Pamment, and Jeff Roy

Badhai's messy, improvised, reciprocal, and recycled practice interacts with a variety of publics, contexts, repertoires, scales, and methodological orientations. We meander through the many possible pathways *badhai* forges, leaning and listening forward while being attentive to how we and our disciplines might be transformed in the process. The dialogue shared through our collaborative authorship remains open-ended in unfinished gestures, attesting to *badhai*'s capacity to be and do multiple things across the transregional *hijrascape* and elsewhere. Straying from the "straight path," the following few pages offer multiple routes for readers to wander with *badhai*:

Badhai ...

Weaves   Cruises   Struts

Opens Doors

Strikes Drums   Claps   Pokes   Whispers   Announces

Touches   Tickles   Celebrates   Aggravates

Fills the Streets

Activates the Senses   Resonates   Triggers   Soothes   Un / Settles

Blesses   Is a Blessing

Transgresses   Subverts   Disrupts

Conforms   Contests / Is Contested   Protests / Is Protest

Forms Relations   Cultivates Interbeing   Collaborates

Co-creates   Pro-creates

Makes Family   Makes *Izzat*   Makes Money

Resists   Persists

Is Resilient   Is Precarious

Be / Longs   Makes Place

Moves Across Borders   Moves Elsewheres

Listens Far   Listens Near Leans In   Leans Out

Voices   Embodies

Takes Risks   Dis / Re / Orients

Is a Rainbow in the Water Bath

Entangles   Loosens Ends

Cycles Rhythms   Bounces off Walls   Encircles

Arranges Sounds   Narrates Movement   Relays Requests

Teases Cisheteronormativity   Decolonizes

Is Multi-Sited   Is Multiscalar   De / Territorializes

Un / Locates   Dis / Places

Improvises   Impresses   Shrouds   Negates

Is Ephemeral   Is Fleeting

Makes Repertoire   Makes Lineage

Is Multi-Temporal   Shifts Margins   Is Affective

Queerly Listens   Sounds Out   Un / Composes

De / Genders   De / Genres   Senses   Is Sensual

Dances   Choreographs   Gestures   Is Unfinished

Un / Binds   Fluctuates

Feels its Way   Makes Intimacies   Mingles

Winks   Wipes a Tear   Shares a Dance

Attaches   Detaches

Intercorporealizes   Multisensorializes   Transculturalizes

Co-Presences   Participates   Is Participatory

Un / Cast(e)s   Whirls   Twinkles   Teaches

Traverses Boundaries   Speculates Is Speculative   Is Spectacular

Pleasures   Praises   Plays

Is a Prayer

Pluralizes Devotion: Hindu / Muslim / Sufi / Wahabi / Shi'a / Sunni / Christian

Voices Goddesses   Embodies Saints

Touches EdgesChanges Forms   Recycles

Mimics   Mimes   Imagines

De / Classes   Announces   Jingles *Ghungroos* Graces *Gurus*

Is Never for the First Time, and Always for the First Time

Makes Demands   Laughs Together   Brings Together   Jests

Showers Money   Tells Stories   Remembers

Sweetens   Sours   Sweats   Struggles   Labors

Flirts   Invites   Is an Invitation

Creates Abundant Possibilities …

Is a Gift

Badhai's abundances constitute its perpetuity, resistance, and survival in the face of post/colonial erasure as well as in this present period of contestations.

Postscript: Futures of *Hijra-Khwaja Sira-Trans* Performance

Kareem Khubchandani

A turn to performance in thinking about *hijra-khwaja sira-trans* life in South Asia is an opportunity to not only lift up the creative labors that are central to *hijra*, *khwaja sira*, *trans*, and queer communities, but to attend also to the complex logics that their artistry invokes and to follow them into the creative worlds their performances fabulate. In order to short circuit the epistemic boundaries around everyday life, cultural performance, and high art, and to think instead about all of these in continuum as forms of artistry that are rehearsed, honed, and deployed toward a variety of ends, we can pay attention to the careful choice-making of *hijra*s and *khwaja sira*s to invent worlds that accommodate their bodies, desires, and pleasures.

Early in my fieldwork on queer nightlife and performance in Bangalore, I was invited by my newly made friends to curate the 2011 annual Pride Mela, an afternoon of performances surrounded by stalls and vendors as part of the Namma Pride and Karnataka Queer Habba festivities. The Mela's first performer was Sneha Prabhu, a *hijra* activist from the documentary *Between the Two* (Dir. Tanvi Talwar, 2011) that I'd watched in Chicago the year prior. Sneha wore a black and gold *lehenga* (long skirt), and kept her long hair loose around her shoulders. When I met her, she was as charming as I had encountered on screen, but I was worried. "You're going first and I don't yet have your music." She read my worry. "Oh! What an honor! I will do a nice dance to bless the stage." She handed the DJ a USB and told him which track to play. Defying my naive expectations of what a "blessing" might look like, Sneha danced to an upbeat Tamil film song, snaking her exposed abdomen, turning her back to the audience and winding her waist, and flaring her skirt as she landed on the ground. Once there she descended backward toward the stage floor to bring attention to her exposed navel, pulsing chest, and luscious hair.

Her performance transformed the venue entirely. Prior to Sneha's arrival on stage, the audience milled about awkwardly, drifting from vendor to vendor. But she drew us in through her dance, and we applauded and hooted for the expertise she showed in setting into motion her hair and skirt with graceful turns and swings of the neck and waist. We showered praise on her for the erotic world she initiated for us as a queer audience, transitioning us from the respectable habitation of the space, orienting us instead toward sexual, feminine, playful, raucous aesthetics. Her performance sanctified the space, teaching us that it was safe to be here in each other's company, in our gaudy fashions and errant flirtations. This was indeed a blessing.

Sneha took responsibility for shaping the event, deciding how she wanted the audience to feel, how she too wanted to feel. She understood that performance has a pedagogical effect, it offers us shared values, affects, and comportments. Her improvised dance number, with song chosen on the spot, does not mean that there was little logic to her performance. Improvised performance is often relegated to the lower rungs of dignity for its unpredictable and seemingly un-studyable nature. However, performance studies teaches us that improvisation is far from spontaneous and irrational movement in the body, it is the sourcing and mixing of accrued repertoires alongside instantaneous responses to the environment. Scholarship on improvisation teaches us that there are many labors, studies, and rehearsals that preceded this play. Studying *badhai* becomes a way of tracking the artistries of *hijra*s and *khwaja sira*s, understanding the many logics and calculations that accrue through rehearsal, everyday life, ritual, and repetition, in order to understand not only what *badhai* does in the present, but what it gestures toward, what worlds it has the capacities to invent. Queer performance studies in particular insists on the values of these momentary worlds, as short as the flare of the skirt or for the duration of the Mela, in suggesting that other worlds, feelings, pleasures, bodies, systems, geographies, relations are possible. To study *badhai*, to think with artistry, helps us understand *hijra*s and *khwaja sira*s as desiring subjects, who hone their crafts and inventive tools that can shape the world around them, that can invent their own futures.

A major contribution of *Badhai: Hijra-Khwaja Sira-Trans Performance across Borders in South Asia* is to teach readers that the work of *hijra-khwaja sira-trans* performance, in ritual, activist, or social settings, does more than extend the longstanding cultural labor associated with *hijra*s and *khwaja sira*s, it does more than fulfill socio-cultural function, especially when those functions look like securing heteronormative futures by blessing babies and marriages. Across Hossain, Pamment, and Roy's chapters, *badhai* emerges as a dynamic performance repertoire that improvises within hostile and friendly conditions to play with and reconfigure social relations for a particularly precarious population of gender-non-normative people. Like Sneha's dance-blessing at the Pride Mela, the *badhai* performances we encounter intensify and disrupt feeling, social bonds, sensorial hegemonies, and gender relations, not only in pursuit of cultural, spiritual, and economic capital, but as a craft of feeling good, fierce, or safe. This book offers an aesthetic ethnography of *badhai* that accounts for its historical and political specificities and describes its functional relevance, but through its rich details it speculates on what *badhai* makes possible when we understand *hijra* and *khwaja sira* song, dance, and even insult as artforms.

I welcome *Badhai: Hijra-Khwaja Sira-Trans Performance across Borders in South Asia* as a necessary contribution to the study of dissident genders in the subcontinent that asks how song and dance practices change with shifting economies and infrastructures, that documents the wickedly funny lyrics of *khwaja sira* repertoires, and that lingers on the vibrant qualities of *hijra* sonic arrangements in addition to their efficacies. Moreover, I welcome this as an urgent contribution to trans studies more broadly, one that quickly moves beyond the notion of gender as performative to actually investigate trans people's aesthetic histories and traditions. Performance, as an object of research, brings into view the nimble labor strategies *hijra*s and *khwaja sira*s draw on alongside the expectations laid down for them by a global NGO industrial complex. Performance insists on feeling and sensation as valuable forms of politicking. Additionally, all three authors use performance as a research method, attending to scenes of *badhai* with their interlocutors. They account for how their bodies function in the field, peeling back the ways that their presence further evidences the stakes of *badhai*. The authors variously function as scribes, photographers, and directors in their field sites, and their interlocutors regularly use them to land a joke or two. Taking performance seriously as a research method, accounting for the ways that their bodies are received, are commented on, feel, and respond during *badhai* visits, Pamment, Roy, and Hossain give us even more insights into what *hijragiri* can look like and why it matters.

Perhaps this book's most unique intervention is its trans-national approach to studying *hijra* and *khwaja sira* performance. Contemporary studies of South Asia tend to be nation bound, and what the authors offer here is a model to think across borders while also understanding the limits that nations place on migrations. Transnational approaches allow scholars to follow the travels of aesthetics, moral regimes, and money, even when bodies (particularly trans bodies) are disciplined at borders. Each of the authors pays careful attention to how *hijra*s and *khwaja sira*s are invited into *and* made abject by specific national imaginaries. At the same time, their careful ethnographies evidence overlapping trends in *hijra* and *khwaja sira* performance across national borders, through the religious plurality of repertoires that draw in Hindu, Sufi, Shi'a, Sunni, and/or Christian material. Certainly the NGO-ization of *hijra* and *khwaja sira* life, particularly under the auspices of global LGBTQ and HIV/AIDS funding, already imbricates Bangladesh, India, and Pakistan. *Hijra* and *khwaja sira* histories, activism, mythologies, and repertoires precede and challenge national formations, and Pamment, Roy, and Hossain's collaborative authorship does urgent work to theorize *badhai* across these borders in ways that are necessary, but are stymied by nationalist projects that manufacture exceptionalism between these three countries.

Badhai is only the beginning. So much more work can still be done to credit the critical knowledge-making practices of *hijra*s and *khwaja sira*s as they navigate precarity, as they celebrate and care for each other and other gender and sexual minorities. Moreover, more work must be done to understand the worlds that *khwaja sira*s and *hijra*s want, the worlds they invent through performance, the worlds they make when they make fun of patriarchs and when their singing voices reverberate into the chaos of their cities. Centering performance is one step toward this, as it allows researchers to pay close attention to the ways that *hijra*s and *khwaja sira*s transfer and mobilize repertoire in the everyday. Thinking across borders is another, as it evidences the abundance of critical cultural practice. And curating and creative production might be a third, making room for *more hijra* and *khwaja sira* performance as Roy and Pamment do through film, theater, and performance engagements with their interlocutors. Queer and trans South Asian studies is far from saturated, and

Badhai: Hijra-Khwaja Sira-Trans Performance across Borders in South Asia teaches us that despite the expansive and sometimes fetishistic body of work on South Asian genders, new approaches are necessary to think with *hijra*s and *khwaja sira*s, and to honor the blessings they offer, the futures they gift us.

Kareem Khubchandani
Tufts University

GLOSSARY

In the heterogeneous linguistic landscapes this book moves through (Bengali, Bhojpuri, Punjabi, Hindi-Urdu, Gujarati, Marathi, Kannada, and Hijra-Farsi or Ulthi) we include a translation of commonly used words—while omitting some obvious terms—using established conventions of Roman transliteration. Some of these terms flow through the hijrascape and/or are derived from regional significations.

Abhinaya leading an audience towards a sentiment through physical gesture in dance.

Bhajan Hindu devotional song.

Birit territorial divisions in Bengali; also *virit*.

Charkha comic song/skit in Punjabi *vadhai*s; literally the spinning wheel.

Chela disciple child/daughter, also *cela*.

Cholla collection of monies and foodstuffs from the marketplaces; also *challa*.

Dera the home, presided over by a *guru*.

Dhamaal ecstatic Sufi dance.

Dholak two-headed drum in North Indian/Urdu contexts, also *dholki* and *dhol*.

Dhol two-headed drum in Bengali, also *dholak* and *dholki*.

Dholki two-headed drum in Punjabi, also *dholak* and *dhol*.

Faqir sufi ascetic.

Gali street or alley.

Gharana network of kinship lineages, also *ghor/ghar*, *silsila*, or *line*.

Ghungroo dancing ankle bells.

Guru teacher or parent.

Guru-nani grandparent, also *guru-dadi* or *nan-guru*.

Harmonium manually pumped reed organ.

Hijragiri *hijra* occupations.

Ilaka area or territory.

Izzat respect or honor.

Jaccha baccha lullaby, also *lori*.

Jajman patrons of *badhai*; literally hosts; also *jodgman*; not to be confused with the *jajmani* system, which is based on reciprocal social and economic arrangements in inter-caste relations.

Khusra *hijra-khwaja sira*, Punjabi.

Kothi contested category with significations that often overlap with *trans* and *hijra*; also *koti*.

Lori lullaby, also *jaccha baccha*.

Manjeera small cymbals, similar to *sheesha*.

Mirasi male musicians who sometimes perform with *toli* groups in areas of North India and Pakistan; literally custodians of heritage.

Naya new.

Qawwali sufi devotional music.

Sehra versified praises sung to wedding celebrants; literally the headdress/garland worn by the groom.

Shadi song versified praises sung to wedding celebrants, also *sehra*.

Sheesha metal clappers, similar to *manjeera*.

Sthai a song's primary theme or refrain, sung in the *madhya saptak*, or middle register.

Taal/tala repeating rhythmic pattern or cycle.

Toli troupe or band.

Vail the act of showering money and giving financial reward to performers, also *variyan*.

Variyan the act of showering money and giving financial reward to performers, also *vail*.

NOTES

Introduction

1 We italicize the prefix "trans" to illuminate its vernacular
   usage, without subsuming other identities under its umbrella.
   Khwaja sira (variant *khwajasara*) is a Mughal-era term (lit.
   "lord of the palace," Abbott 2020: 8; see also Hinchy 2019:
   23–4; Khan 2019). In Pakistan there are regional variants,
   such as *moorat*, *faqir* (variant *fakir*) which is used particularly
   in the South (Kasmani 2012; Pamment 2019a: 304), *bugga*
   in Balochistan (Naqvi and Mujtaba 1997), and *khusra* in
   the Punjab. Other transgender and gender nonconforming
   communities possess distinct yet overlapping relational
   networks and practices, such as the *thirunungai*s of Tamil
   Nadu (Craddock 2018; Nataraj 2019; Tom and Menon
   2021; Vasudevan 2020), *siva sakhti*s of Andra Pradesh, and
   *jogappa*s or *jogta*s of North Karnataka, Andra Pradesh, and
   Maharashtra (Roy 2015a: 15; Dutta, Khan, and Lorway 2019;
   see Dutta et al. 2022).

2 While we employ the term *hijrascape* to point to the
   interconnected networks of communication across *hijra-khwaja
   sira-trans* relationalities spanning boundaries of nation, we also
   acknowledge the politics and limitations of naming which at
   times reduce movements and flows. Further, the pronouns we
   use throughout the book reflect the heterogeneity of gender
   subjectivities of *hijra-khwaja sira-trans* people we have worked
   with in our various locations.

3 At least one of the lineages noted by Reddy—Lashkari or
   Lashkarwale (Reddy 2005: 9–10)—is found in places such as
   Western Maharashtra (Roy 2015a: 10) and Pakistan, while
   other lineages may not have as many prominent supraregional
   or transregional referents, such as the Delhi-based Rai *gharana*

and the Western Maharashtrian Punewale and Bhindi Bazaar *gharana*s. Indeed, some lineages span national boundaries; Mohini and Shazani (related to Sujan in Delhi) are notable in the Punjab, a region which crosses India and Pakistan; and the Shambazaria, Ghunguria, and Machuya lineages traverse Bangladesh and areas of West Bengal. The *ghar*s in Delhi, according to *hijra*s in Bangladesh, are Rai, Sujania, Kallyani, and Mandi. Many *hijra*s from Bangladesh join those *ghar*s when they work there but they may also change back into the Bangladeshi lineages when they return.

4 In Pakistan Mai Nandi is described as one originary *hijra* figure, which some (though not all) conflate with Bahuchara Mata (Abbas and Pir 2016: 162–3).

5 In North India and some parts of Pakistan, the instrument is referred to as the *dholak*. In Bangladesh, the drum is called *dhol*, whereas in Punjab, *dholki* and occasionally *dholak* are used interchangeably. In some contexts, the terms *dholak*, *dholki*, and *dhol* may also denote differently sized drums, the largest being the *dhol* and the smallest being the *dholki*.

6 Archival references from Nick Abbott, Shahnaz Khan, and Claire Pamment's collaborative work, sponsored by SSHRC (2014).

7 "Dancing in public of eunuchs in female clothing afterwards leads to sodomy, therefore it should be prohibited" (Simson 1866; in Hinchy 2014: 281).

8 In the colonial archive, the Extra Assistant Commissioner Rai Harsahari warns that "in the matter of the rejoicing on the birth of a son [the anti-*hijra* legislation will] interfere with a very old Hindu custom" (in Stokes 1870). This religio-cultural advocacy is marginalized, and Rai Harsahari is quickly dismissed as an "orthodox, conservative and somewhat bigoted Hindu" (MacAndrew in ibid.).

9 For a performance-based critique of the interaction of the colonial gaze in contemporary and historical surveillance regimes, see *Teesri Dhun* (Pamment et al. 2015; Pamment et al. 2021: 223–4).

10 By the mid-1990s in some regions of South Asia, *kothi* (variant *koti*) as "males who show varying degrees of femininity"

emerged as one of the primary subcategories of MSM on the heels of HIV activism (Reddy 2018). Within the schemes of government and NGO recognition, *kothi* became an "authentic" South Asian variant under the MSM umbrella, under which *hijra* was subsumed. This movement exposed the rifts of class, gender, sexuality, and cultural authenticity, as evidenced by Cohen's chapter on the "Kothi Wars" (2005). Dutta discusses how the distinction between *kothi* and *hijra* reinforces "intracommunity tensions while eliding overlaps and fluidity" (2013: 509). Turning away from certain essentialisms, we understand *kothi* to be a contested category with significations that often overlap with *trans* and *hijra*.

11 In 2009, Section 377 was nullified by the Supreme Court, and in 2013, reinstated with support from religious leaders. India struck down Section 377 for the second time in 2018.

12 For three films on the religious, political, and performance practices taking place at Koovagam, see *Koovagam (Part 1)*, *Meet Gopi (Koovagam Part 2)"* and *The Importance of Miss Koovagam*, in *Music in Liminal Spaces* (Roy 2012–13).

Chapter 1

1 Throughout this chapter, I have used pseudonyms for all my interlocutors to protect their identities, except when they wished for their real names to be used.

2 Although the government of Bangladesh recognized *hijra*s as a separate gender/sex through a policy decision in 2013, a gazette notification to that effect was issued by the government in 2014.

3 I use "they/them/their" throughout this chapter to demonstrate the context-specific and fluid nature of *hijra* gender presentation.

4 Throughout this chapter, all translations into English from Bangla are mine unless otherwise specified.

5 Bangladesh is a Muslim majority country with a sizable Sufi following. Although Hindus are a minority, the categorial

oppositions of Hindu versus Muslims are often collapsed in practice, which many reformist and militant Islamist groups begrudge. Muslim *hijra*s in Bangladesh often situate their Hindu-marked cosmology and practices within the framework of an open and transcendent Islam. For more on Bangladeshi Islam and its polyvocality, see Bertocci 2001 and Van Schendel 2007.

6 *Jodgman* is a *hijra* word in Bangladesh similar to *jajman* in Pakistan as used by Pamment in this book. *Hijra*s in Bangladesh employ *jodgman* to signify the mainstream majority, publics, and ordinary citizens that they approach for *badhai* and *cholla*.

7 Similar definition also figures in the official website of the Ministry of Social Welfare of Bangladesh. See for example https://www.msw.gov.bd (accessed October 1, 2021).

8 The word used in this chapter, however, is transgender and it is used exclusively to refer to *hijra*s.

9 Such boundaries are not, however, always rigidly defined, since community members often participate in reciprocal economy by giving money on special occasions or whenever they feel they should, regardless of the sources of income.

10 Even the person without a penis and scrotum was declared to be genetically male since they had their penis and scrotum removed.

11 Details on the screening procedure and the certificate issued in support of one's *hijra* status are discussed in the "Implementation Manual of Livelihood Development of Hijra 2013," http://www.msw.gov.bd/sites/default/files/files/msw.portal. gov.bd/policies/25925cec_e191_4bed_ab10_9d2ffc86b06f/ Hizra-Manual-090113.pdf (accessed June 3, 2022). It is also noteworthy that the Ministry of Social Welfare keeps changing some of their descriptions on the website from time to time.

Chapter 2

1 I use the Punjabi "*vadhai*" to signal the heterogeneity of these practices. Translations of performances and interviews are from Punjabi and/or Urdu, with the assistance of Anaya Rahimi, Nukhbat Malik, and Sarmad Sehbai.

2 Pakistan's Transgender Persons (Protection of Rights) Act entails legal recognition and protections for transgender people according to self-identification: whether "intersex or khunsa," "eunuch," "transgender man, transgender woman or khwaja sira or any person whose gender identity and/or gender expression differs from the social norms and cultural expectations based on the sex they were assigned at the time of their birth" (National Assembly of Pakistan 2018).

3 The short film *Vadhai: A Gift* (Pamment et al. 2019c) includes some of the performances and interviews of Amber's *toli* featured in this chapter.

4 For a *charkha* performance by Reema and Sana in their *ilaka*, see Pamment 2019a: 308.

5 Bebo Haider, one of the *khwaja sira* tax collection employees, explains that the *khwaja sira* recruits neither came from *toli* backgrounds nor drew on its repertoires, and were subjected to precarious working conditions (2014).

6 While performers often spoke of *bad-dua* in my early field work (2008–13), many performers were keen to disassociate from this concept in my later research (2014–19).

Chapter 3

1 As Dylan Robinson observes in their work with the First Nations peoples of Canada, in settler colonial listening— *shxwelítemelh xwélala:m* in Halq'eméylem words, or "hungry listening"—the subjective experience of what and how we hear are directly composed by a writing process that demands the rendering of music and sound as objects (2020: 15). The term "de-composing" stems from Chérie Rivers Ndaliko and Petna Ndaliko Katondolo's work on de-composing the colonial gaze through decolonial filmmaking in the Democratic Republic of the Congo (2016; 2019).

2 Yvon Bonenfant describes queer listening as a "listening out for, reach[ing] towards, the disoriented or differently oriented other [...] listening out through the static produced by not-queer

emanations of vocalic bodies" (2010: 78). Elsewhere, I explore the possibilities of being "queerly sincere and sincerely queer" to describe the deep and persistent ways music can be felt and sensed in collaborative work, and how such work disrupts conventional hierarchies of authority and authenticity that frame transnational queer relationality (Roy 2019a), drawing on the dialectic between authenticity and sincerity in ethnographic practice addressed by John L. Jackson (2005; 2010).

3 "Movements of narration" expands Kasmani's "scenes of narration" (2017) through a particular focus on the ways music, sound, and other performance productions are arranged as they emerge from and move through different registers of fragmented knowledge, memory, and intimacy. I have used a similar approach to writing "scenes" in my ethnography of a *hijra jalsa* in Maharashtra, to explore how *badhai, qawwali*, and other performances extend beyond the production of gesture and sound to include practices of place-making, collaboration, and belonging. With a focus on the progressive ordering of *badhai* music and other musical events, that text examines how such performances lead to shared experience of *sultana* (Racy 2004)—the ecstatic moment of disorientation in which participants find themselves untethered from conventional formations of self-understanding and connected to one another through music and dance (Roy 2017).

4 This is critical for the purposes of our collaboratively authored transregional *badhai* study, since thin, cruisy, and queer writing articulates the fragmented connections, resonances, dissonances, flows, and fissures of *badhai* travel across the borders in the *hijrascape*.

5 Please refer to the following URL: https://www.jeff-roy.com/badhai.

6 At this moment, I am transported elsewhere, to *badhai* sonic arrangements inside *dera* spaces in Maharashtra, Gujarat, and other parts of Uttar Pradesh, where vocalists sing—or otherwise "sound out"—through uniquely stylized inflections that slip into and disrupt the sonic space of the rooms we inhabit. Each voice is uniquely inflected, and the arrangements they form are differently organized and textured, with vocalic productions oriented not toward the repetition or replication of finely crafted

sounds, toward mimetic virtuosity of monophonic melody, but toward an attunement to sounding out and listening beyond what is recognizably classical or musically "conventional." Together, the voices of the lead and secondary singers sound urgent, voluminous, angular yet magnetizing in *madhya saptak*, interacting with each other in dissonance.

7 Elsewhere, I discuss "aural osmosis" and other immersive embodied experiences in the learning of *badhai* song in the *dera* and across various *gharana*s (Roy 2015a).

8 See Jack Halberstam's *The Queer Art of Failure* (2011).

REFERENCES

Abbas, Qaisar, and Ghiasuddin Pir (2016), "History of the Invisible: A People's History of the Transgendered Community of Lahore." *THAAP*: 162–75.

Abbott, Nicholas (2020), "'In that One the Ālif is Missing': Eunuchs and the Politics of Masculinity in Early Colonial North India." *Journal of the Economic and Social History of the Orient* 63, no. 1–2: 73–116.

AFP (2013), "Pakistani transgender candidate to run for office." *Dawn News*, February 25. https://www.dawn.com/news/788630/i.dawn.com (accessed January 3, 2022).

Ahmed, Jamil (2014), "Designs of Living in the Contemporary Theatre of Bangladesh." In *Mapping South Asia through Contemporary Theatre*, edited by Ashis Sengupta, 135–76. London: Palgrave Macmillan.

Ahmed Murtaza (2010), "Hum Sab Umeed Se Hain New Song (9th January 2010)." *YouTube*, January 9. https://www.youtube.com/watch?v=gkBa9Xbvmr8 (accessed November 19, 2021).

Ahmed, Nizam (2011), "Bangladeshi beggars to stay off streets during World Cup." *Reuters*, February 2. https://www.reuters.com/article/idINIndia-54600420110202 (accessed November 20, 2020).

Ahmed, Sara (2004), *The Cultural Politics of Emotion*. London: Routledge.

Ahmed, Sara (2006), *Queer Phenomenology: Orientations, Objects, Others*. Durham, NC: Duke University Press.

Ahmed, Sara (2013), "Making Feminist Points." *feministkillsjoys*, September 11. https://feministkilljoys.com/2013/09/11/making-feminist-points/ (accessed November 1, 2021).

Ahmed, Sara (2014), *Willful Subjects*. Durham, NC: Duke University Press.

Ahsen, Saud bin (2019), "Transgenders in Pakistan." *Daily Times*, September 8. https://dailytimes.com.pk/461958/transgenders-in-pakistan-part-i/ (accessed September 8, 2019).

Alexander, M. Jacqui (2006), *Pedagogies of Crossing*. Durham, NC: Duke University Press.

Ali, Nayyab (2018), "Coverage of my election compaign [*sic*] ... Samaa." *YouTube*, May 27. https://www.facebook.com/nayyabokara/videos/609709506067865 (accessed September 8, 2019).

Amber, Goshi, and Sheela Maham, with Aamar Ali, Faisal Sadiq Ali, Shabbir (2019), *Vadhai* performances and conversations with Claire Pamment and Anaya Rahimi, Bhaghvanpura, Lahore, October 7.

Amine, Khalid, and Marvin Carlson (2008), "'Al-Halqa' in Arabic Theatre: An Emerging Site of Hybridity." *Theatre Journal* 60, no. 1: 71–85.

Amine, Khalid, and Marvin Carlson (2012), *The Theatres of Morocco, Algeria and Tunisia*. London: Palgrave Macmillan.

Anderson, Benedict ([1983] 1991), *Imagined Communities: Reflections on the Origin and Spread of Nationalism*. London; New York: Verso.

Antara, Nawaz Farhin (2021), "Breaking down barriers, leaping across prejudice." *Dhaka Tribune*, February 4. https://www.dhakatribune.com/bangladesh/2021/02/04/breaking-down-barriers-leaping-across-prejudice (accessed June 20, 2021).

Appadurai, Arjun (1996), *Modernity at Large: Cultural Dimensions of Globalization*. Minneapolis: University of Minnesota Press.

APWG (After Performance Working Group) (2016), "After Performance: On Transauthorship." *Performance Research* 21, no. 5: 35–6.

Arondekar, Anjali (2009), *For the Record: On Sexuality and the Colonial Archive in India*. Durham, NC: Duke University Press.

Arondekar, Anjali (2021), Remarks for the Session "Historical Gaps/Sexual Liminalities." 5th Queer Symposium at the 49th Annual Conference on South Asia.

Arondekar, Anjali (2023), *Abundance: Sexuality and Historiography*. Durham, NC: Duke University Press.

Arondekar, Anjali, and Geeta Patel (2016), "Area Impossible." *Gay Lesbian Quarterly* 22, no. 2: 151–71.

Arondekar, Anjali, Ann Cvetkovich, Christina B. Hanhardt, Regina Kunzel, Tavia Nyong'O, Juana María Rodríguez, and Susan Stryker (2015), "Queering Archives: A Roundtable Discussion." *Radical History Review* 122: 211–31.

Bacchetta, Paola (2010), "Decolonial Praxis: Enabling Intranational and Transnational Queer Coalition Building. Paola Bacchetta Interviewed by Marcelle Maese-Cohen." *Qui Parle: Critical Humanities and Social Science* 18, no. 2: 147–92.

Balance, Christine Bacareza (2016), *Tropical Renditions: Making Musical Scenes in Filipino America*. Durham, NC: Duke University Press.

Bakshi, Sandeep (2020), "The Decolonial Eye/I: Decolonial Enunciations of Queer Diasporic Practices." *Interventions* 22, no. 4: 533–51.

Banerji, Anurima (2010), "Paratopias of Performance: The Choreographic Practices of Chandralekha." In *Planes of Composition: Dance and the Global*, edited by Andre Lepecki and Jenn Joy, 346–71. Kolkata: Seagull Press.

Batool, Farida (2004), *Figure: The Popular and the Political in Pakistan*. Lahore: ASR.

BBC (2021), "Bangladesh's first transgender news reader makes debut." *BBC News*, March 9. https://www.bbc.co.uk/news/world-asia-56332730 (accessed July 19, 2021).

Bertocci, Peter J. (2001), "Islam and the Social Construction of the Bangladesh Countryside." In *Understanding Bengal Muslims: Interpretive Essays*, edited by Ahmed Rafiuddin, 71–85. New Delhi: Oxford University Press.

Bharucha, Rustom (1993), *Theatre and the World: Performance and the Politics of Culture*. London; New York: Routledge.

Bhattacharya, Sayan (2019), "The Transgender Nation and its Margins: The Many Lives of the Law." *South Asia Multidisciplinary Academic Journal* 20: 1–19.

Bholi (2019), Interview with Claire Pamment. Lahore, October 26.

Billard, Tomas J., and Sam Nesfield (2021), "(Re)making 'Transgender' Identities in Global Media and Popular Culture." In *Trans Lives in a Globalizing World*, edited by J. M. Ryan, 66–90. London: Routledge.

Boellstorff, Tom, Mauro Cabral, Micha Cárdenas, Trystan Cotten, Eric A. Stanley, Kalaniopua Young, and Aren Z. Aizura (2014), "Decolonizing Transgender: A Roundtable Discussion." *TSQ: Transgender Studies Quarterly* 1, no. 3: 419–39.

Bonenfant, Yvon (2010), "Queer Listening to Queer Vocal Timbres." *Performance Research* 5, no. 3: 74–80.

Boone, Jon (2016), "Pakistan transgender leader calls for end to culture of 'gurus.'" *The Guardian*, December 25. https://www.theguardian.com/society/2016/dec/25/pakistan-transgender-leader-culture-of-gurus–nadeem-kashish (accessed December 1, 2019).

Bor, Joep (1986–7), *The Voice of the Sarangi*. Bombay: National Center for the Performing Arts.

Bukhari, Anmol, and Ashee (2019), Interview with Claire Pamment. Lahore, October 31.

Burnes, Alxr (1829), "Eunuchs or Pawyus of Cutch." September 5, 1829. In BL/Mss Eur. D155.

Butler, Judith (1988), "Performative Acts and Gender Constitution: An Essay in Phenomenology and Feminist Theory." *Theatre Journal* 40, no. 4: 519–31.

Butt, Ashee (2020), Facebook video post, February 4. https://www.facebook.com/ashee.gee/videos/1815564945242630/?t=547 (accessed February 5, 2020).

Carlson, Marvin (2001), *The Haunted Stage: The Theatre as Memory Machine*. Ann Arbor: University of Michigan Press.

Chakravorty, Pallabi (2008), *Bells of Change: Kathak Dance, Women and Modernity in India*. Chicago: The University of Chicago Press.

Chandola, Tripta (2010), "Listening in to Others: In Between Noise and Silence." PhD Diss., Queensland University of Technology, Brisbane.

Chandola, Tripta (2011), "Listening into Others: Moralising the Soundscapes in Delhi." *International Development Planning Review* 34, no. 4: 391–408.

Cheema, Usman (2009), "Politicians, relatives own 50pc of countrys [*sic*] sugar factories." *The Nation*, August 23. https://nation.com.pk/23-Aug-2009/politicians-relatives-own-50pc-of-countrys-sugar-factories (accessed November 19, 2021).

Chowdhury, Sanjana (2020), "Transgender in Bangladesh: First school opens for trans students." *BBC*, November 6. https://www.bbc.com/news/world-asia-54838305 (accessed August 20, 2021).

Cohen, Lawrence (1995), "The Pleasures of Castration: The Postoperative Status of Hijras, Jankhas and Academics." In *Sexual Nature, Sexual Culture*, edited by Paul R. Abramson and Steven D. Pinkerton, 276–304. Chicago: The University of Chicago Press.

Cohen, Lawrence (2005), "The Kothi Wars: AIDS Cosmopolitanism and the Morality of Classification." In *Sex in Development: Science, Sexuality, and Morality in Global Perspective*, edited by Stacy Leigh Pigg and Vincanne Adams, 269–304. Durham, NC: Duke University Press.

Coke Studio (2018a), "Coke Studio Season 11| Hum Dekhenge." *YouTube*, July 22. https://www.youtube.com/watch?v=unOqa2tnzSM (accessed August 5, 2018).

Coke Studio (2018b), "Coke Studio Season 11| Baalkada| Lucky, Naghma & Jimmy Khan." *YouTube*, August 10. https://www.youtube.com/watch?v=LOojBeYVhDQ (accessed August 5, 2018).

Coke Studio (2018c), "Coke Studio Season 11| BTS| Baalkada| Lucky, Naghma & Jimmy Khan." *YouTube*, August 10. https://www.youtube.com/watch?v=GU-holu9uWA (accessed August 5, 2018).

Conquergood, Dwight (2002), "Performance Studies: Interventions and Radical Research." *TDR: The Drama Review* 46, no. 2: 145–56.

Conquergood, Dwight (2013), *Cultural Struggles: Performance, Ethnography, Praxis*. Edited and with a critical introduction by E. Patrick Johnson. Ann Arbor: University of Michigan Press.

Cooper, Timothy P. A. (2021), "3D *Ziyarat*: Lenticularity and Technologies of the Moving Image in Material and Visual Piety." *Material Religion* 17, no. 3: 291–316.

Craddock, Elaine (2018), "Recalibrating (Field)work." *QED: A Journal in GLBTQ Worldmaking* 5, no. 3: 100–16.

Daily Sun (2018), "Nuisance in public places by hijras sharply rising." *Daily Sun*, August 16. https://www.daily-sun.com/post/329943/Nuisance-in-public-places-by-hijras-sharply-rising (accessed November 30, 2020).

Dawn (2019), "'We are owning you': PM Imran launches health scheme for transgender community." *Dawn*, December 30. https://www.dawn.com/news/1525268 (accessed November 19, 2021).

Debnath, Bipul K. (2017), "Begging profession." *The Independent*, July 14. http://m.theindependentbd.com/magazine/details/103831/Begging-Profession (accessed November 25, 2020).

Devnath, Bishakha (2019), "Beggars' rehabilitation: Govt failure writ large." *The Daily Star*, April 25. https://www.thedailystar.net/frontpage/news/beggars-rehabilitation-govt-failure-writ-large-1734364 (accessed November 30, 2020).

Drewal, Margaret Thompson (2003), "Improvisation as Participatory Performance: Egungun Masked Dancers in the Yoruba Tradition." In *Taken by Surprise: A Dance Improvisation Reader*, edited by Ann Cooper Albright and David Gere, 119–34. Middletown, CT: Wesleyan University Press.

Dutta, Aniruddha (2012), "An Epistemology of Collusion: *Hijra*, *Kothi* and the Historical (Dis)continuity of Gender/Sexual Identities in Eastern India." *Gender & History* 24, no. 3: 825–49.

Dutta, Aniruddha (2013), "Legible Identities and Legitimate Citizens: The Globalization of Transgender and Subjects of HIV-AIDS Prevention in Eastern India." *International Feminist Journal of Politics* 15, no. 4: 494–514.

Dutta, Aniruddha (forthcoming), "The Freedom to Dance: Performance and Impersonation in Lagan." In *Mimetic Desires: Impersonation and Guising across South Asia*, edited by Harshita Mruthinti Kamath and Pamela Lothspeich. Hawaii: University of Hawaii Press.

Dutta, Aniruddha, and Raina Roy (2014), "Decolonizing Transgender in India: Some Reflections." *TSQ: Transgender Studies Quarterly* 1, no. 3: 320–37.

Dutta, Aniruddha, Adnan Hossain, and Claire Pamment (2022), "Re-Mapping the *Hijras* of South Asia: Toward Transregional and Global Flows." In *Handbook of the Changing World LGBTQ Map*, edited by Stanley D. Brunn and Marianne Blidon, 85–103. Cham, Switzerland: Springer.

Dutta, Sumit, Shamshad Khan, and Robert Lorway (2019), "Following the Divine: An Ethnographic Study of Structural Violence among Transgender *Jogappas* in South India." *Culture, Health & Sexuality* 21, no. 11: 1240–56.

Ellawala, Themal, and Jeff Roy (2021), "Mind the Gap: Queer Erasure and Abundance in Contentious Times." 5th Queer Symposium at the 49th Annual Conference on South Asia.

Escobar, Arturo (1995), *Encountering Development: The Making and Unmaking of the Third World*. Princeton, NJ: Princeton University Press.

Fabian, Johannes ([1983] 2014), *Time and the Other: How Anthropology Makes Its Object*. New York: Columbia University Press.

Faqir, Sanam (2014), Phone interview with Nukhbat Malik and Claire Pamment. April 19.

Feinberg, Leslie (1996), *Transgender Warriors: Making History from Joan of Arc to Dennis Rodman*. Boston, MA: Beacon Press.

Ferdous, Rubayat, Rita Voumik, Rafiqul Islam Royal, Sajeeb Sarkar, Chittironjon Shil, and Nusrat Jahan (2019), "Hijra songskriti." [Culture of hijra]. In *Hijra Sobdokosh* [Encyclopedia of hijra], edited by Selina Hossain, 110–53. Dhaka: Somoy Prakason.

Gannon, Kathy (2020), "Transgender Pakistanis find solace in a church of their own." *Associated Press*, November 25. https://apnews.com/article/international-news-karachi-pakistan-south-asia-asia-f7dec23fd300282b3570420c01a5fac8 (accessed December 5, 2020).

Gaston, Anne-Marie (1996), *Bharata Natyam: From Temple to Theatre*. New Delhi: Manohar.

General Economics Division Planning Commission Government of the People's Republic of Bangladesh (2010), *Outline Perspective Plan of Bangladesh 2010–2021: Making Vision 2021 a Reality*. Dhaka: Government of the People's Republic of Bangladesh, June. https://unctad.org/system/files/non-official-document/dtl_eWeek2018c03-bangladesh_en.pdf (accessed October 1, 2021).

General Economics Division Planning Commission Government of the People's Republic of Bangladesh (2015), *National Social Security Strategy (NSSS) of Bangladesh*. Dhaka: Government of the People's Republic of Bangladesh, July. http://extwprlegs1.fao.org/docs/pdf/bgd167449.pdf (accessed October 1, 2021).

Gogi, Naghma (2019), Interview with Claire Pamment. Lahore, August 7.

Gopinath, Gayatri (2005), *Impossible Desires: Queer Diasporas and South Asian Public Cultures*. Durham, NC: Duke University Press.

Gopinath, Gayatri (2018), *Unruly Visions: The Aesthetic Practices of Queer Diaspora*. Durham, NC: Duke University Press.

Goshi and Maham (2019), Interview with Claire Pamment and Anaya Malik. Lahore, September 15.

Haider, Bebo (2014), Interview with Claire Pamment and Shahnaz Khan. Lahore, January 17.

Halberstam, Jack (2011), *The Queer Art of Failure*. Durham, NC: Duke University Press.

Hall, Kira (1997), "'Go Suck Your Husband's Sugarcane!' Hijras and the Use of Sexual Insult." In *Queerly Phrased: Language, Gender and Sexuality*, edited by Anna Livia and Kira Hall, 430–60. New York: Oxford University Press.

Hamzić, Vanja (2019), "The *Dera* Paradigm: Homecoming of the Gendered Other." *EthnoScripts* 21 no. 1: 34–57.

Hiltebeitel, Alf (1980), "Śiva, the Goddess, and the Disguises of the Pāṇḍavas and Draupadi." *History of Religions* 20 no. 1/2: 147–74.

Hiltebeitel, Alf (1995), "Dying Before the Mahabharata War: Martial and Transsexual Body-Building for Aravan." *The Journal of Asian Studies* 54, no. 2: 447–73.

Hinchy, Jessica (2014), "Obscenity, Moral Contagion and Masculinity: Hijras in Public Space in Colonial North India." *Asian Studies Review* 38, no. 2: 274–94.

Hinchy, Jessica (2019), *Governing Gender and Sexuality in Colonial India: The Hijra, c.1850–1900*. Cambridge: Cambridge University Press.

Hindustan Times (2015), "Mumbai Transgenders Show the True Meaning of Freedom." *Hindustan Times*, August 14. https://www.hindustantimes.com/mumbai/mumbai-s-transgenders-show-the-true-meaning-of-freedom/story-emLoLh1nn7RNWq6RpfxnSJ.html (accessed November 1, 2021).

Hirschkind, Charles (2006), *The Ethical Soundscape: Cassette Sermons and Islamic Counterpublics*. New York: Columbia University Press.

Hobart, R. T. 1875, Letter from Deputy Inspector-General of Police, to Inspector-General of Police, North-Western Provinces, (No. 396C.), May 4 in BL/IOR/P/97.

Hossain, Adnan (2012), "Beyond Emasculation: Being Muslim and Becoming *Hijra* in South Asia." *Asian Studies Review* 36, no. 4: 495–513.

Hossain, Adnan (2017), "The Paradox of Recognition: *Hijra*, Third Gender and Sexual Rights in Bangladesh." *Culture, Health & Sexuality* 19, no. 12: 1418–31.

Hossain, Adnan (2018), "De-Indianizing Hijra: Intraregional Effacements and Inequalities in South Asian Queer Space." *TSQ: Transgender Studies Quarterly* 5, no. 3: 321–31.

Hossain, Adnan (2021), *Beyond Emasculation: Pleasure and Power in the Making of Hijra in Bangladesh*. Cambridge: Cambridge University Press.

Hossain, Adnan (2022), "Metaphor of Contagion: Impact of Covid-19 on the Hijras in Bangladesh." In *COVID-19*

Assemblages: Queer and Feminist Ethnographies from South Asia, edited by Niharika Banerjea, Paul Boyce, and Rohit K. Dasgupta, 100–6. London; New York: Routledge.

Hossain, Adnan, and Serena Nanda (2020), "Globalization and Change among the Hijras of South Asia." In *Trans Lives in a Globalizing World*, edited by J. Michael Ryan, 34–49. London: Routledge.

Hossain, Adnan, and Sino Esthappan (2021), "Trans and Hijra Lives in the Covid 19 Era." TNN, VU Amsterdam and ShareNet International. https://share-netinternational.org/wp-content/uploads/2021/03/Hossain-et-al.-2021-final.pdf (accessed July 1, 2021).

Igualdad, Exige (2018), "13 Trans Candidates Are Running in Pakistan's Elections This Week." *Globalcitizen*, July 24. https://www.globalcitizen.org/es/content/pakistan-transgender-candidates-elections/ (accessed November 19, 2021).

India TV (2015), "Transgenders Singing Jana Gana Mana Will Give You Goosebumps." *IndiaTVNews.com*, August 13. https://www.indiatvnews.com/news/india/transgenders-singing-jana-gana-mana-will-give-you-goosebumps-53690.html (accessed January 15, 2021).

Iqbal, Qasim (2018), Personal correspondence. *Facebook Messenger*, December 28.

Jackson, John L. (2005), *Real Black: Adventures in Racial Sincerity*. Chicago: The University of Chicago Press.

Jackson, John. L. (2010), "On Ethnographic Sincerity." *Current Anthropology* 51, no. S2: 279–87.

Jagiella, Leyla (2022), *Among the Eunuchs: A Muslim Transgender Journey*. London: Hurst.

Kabutri (2019), Interview with Claire Pamment and Anaya Rahimi. Lahore, October 19.

Kamath, Harshita Mruthinti (2019), *Impersonations: The Artifice of Brahmin Masculinity in South Indian Dance*. Berkeley: University of California Press.

Kang, Akhil (2016a), "Casteless-ness in the Name of Caste." *Round Table India*, March 4. https://roundtableindia.co.in/index.php?option=com_content&view=article&id=8491:casteless-ness-in-the-name-of-caste&catid=119:feature&Itemid=132 (accessed November 15, 2021).

Kang, Akhil (2016b), "Queering Dalit." *Tanqeed*, October. https://www.tanqeed.org/2016/10/queering-dalit-tq-salon/ (accessed November 15, 2021).

Kapchan, Deborah A. (1995), "Performance." *The Journal of American Folklore* 108, no. 430: 479–508.

Kapchan, Deborah A. (2007), *Traveling Spirit Masters: Moroccan Gnawa Trance and Music in the Global Marketplace*. Middletown, CT: Wesleyan University Press.

Kapchan, Deborah (2017), "Listening Acts: Witnessing the Pain (and Praise) of Others." In *Theorizing Sound Writing*, edited by Deborah Kapchan, 277–93. Middletown, CT: Wesleyan University Press.

Kashish, Nadeem (2020a), *Facebook* post, January 8. https://www.facebook.com/nadeem.kashish.3/videos/1206176892906702 (accessed January 12, 2020).

Kashish, Nadeem (2020b), *Facebook* post, January 11. https://www.facebook.com/nadeem.kashish.3/videos/1206917629499295 (accessed January 12, 2020).

Kasmani, Omar (2012), "Of Discontinuity and Difference: Gender and Embodiment among Fakirs of Sehwan Sharif*." *Oriente Modern* 92, no. 2: 439–57.

Kasmani, Omar (2017), "Audible Spectres: The Sticky Shia Sonics of Sehwan" [formally adapted version of the first text from October 2017]. *History of Emotions – Insights into Research*. http://dx.doi.org/10.14280/08241.54.v2

Kasmani, Omar (2021a), "Futuring Trans* in Pakistan: Timely Reflections." *TSQ: Transgender Studies Quarterly* 8, no. 1: 96–112.

Kasmani, Omar (2021b), "Feeling Sufis: An Essay on Intimate Religion in Berlin." In *Urban Religious Events: Public Spirituality in Contested Spaces*, edited by Paul Bramadat, Mar Griera, Julia Martínez-Ariño, and Marian Burchardt, 189–202. London: Bloomsbury Academic.

Kasmani, Omar (2021c), "Thin, Cruisy, Queer: Writing through Affect." In *Gender and Genre in Ethnographic Writing*, edited by Elisabeth Tauber and Dorothy L. Zinn, 163–88. London: Palgrave Macmillan.

Kasmani, Omar, Pavithra Prasad, and Jeff Roy, co-chairs (2019), "Journeys ←→ Queer Elsewheres: A Symposium on South Asian

Imaginaries." 4th Queer Symposium at the Annual Conference on South Asia.

Kasmani, Omar, Nasima Selim, Hansjörg Dilger, and Dominik Mattes (2020), "Introduction: Elsewhere Affects and the Politics of Engagement across Religious Life-Worlds." *Religion and Society* 11, no. 1: 92–104.

Katondolo, Petna Ndaliko, director (2019), *Matata*, film. Produced by Chérie Rivers Ndaliko.

Katz, Max (2017), *Lineage of Loss: Counternarratives of North Indian Music*. Middletown, CT: Wesleyan University Press.

Kersenboom, Saskia (1987), *Nityasumangali: Devadasi Tradition in South India*. Delhi: Motilal Banarsidass Publishers.

Kersenboom, Saskia (1995), "Judiciary, Social Reform and Debate on 'Religious Prostitution' in Colonial India." *Economic and Political Weekly* 30, no. 43–WS: 59–65.

Khan, Faris (2014), "Khwaja Sira: 'Transgender' Activism and Transnationality in Pakistan." In *South Asia in the World: An Introduction*, edited by Susan S. Wadley, 170–84. New York: Routledge.

Khan, Faris (2019), "Institutionalizing an Ambiguous Category: 'Khwaja Sira' Activism, the State, and Sex/Gender Regulation in Pakistan." *Anthropological Quarterly* 92 no. 4: 1135–71.

Khubchandani, Kareem (2020), *Ishtyle: Accenting Gay Indian Nightlife*. Ann Arbor, MI: University of Michigan Press.

LaBelle, Brandon (2021), *Acoustic Justice: Listening, Performativity, and the Work of Reorientation*. New York: Bloomsbury.

Lieder, K. Frances (2018), "Performing Loitering: Feminist Protest in the Indian City." *TDR: The Drama Review* 62, no. 3: 145–61.

Madison, D. Soyini (2007), "Co-Performative Witnessing." *Cultural Studies* 21, no. 6: 826–31.

Madison, D. Soyini (2011), "The Labor of Reflexivity." *Cultural Studies ←→ Critical Methodologies* 11, no. 2: 129–38.

McKittrick, Katherine (2021), *Dear Science and Other Stories*. Durham, NC: Duke University Press.

Medhuri, Avanti (2008), "Transfiguration of Indian/Asian Dance in the UK: Bharatanatyam in Global Contexts." *Asian Theatre Journal* 25, no 2: 298–328.

Menon, Jisha (2013), *The Performance of Nationalism: India, Pakistan, and the Memory of Partition*. Cambridge: Cambridge University Press.

Merleau-Ponty, Maurice (2002), *Phenomenology of Perception*, translated by Colin Smith. London: Routledge & Kegan Paul.

Meyer, Moe (2010), *An Archeology of Posing: Essays on Camp, Drag, and Sexuality*. Chicago: Macater Press.

Ministry of Social Welfare, People's Republic of Bangladesh (2018), *The Livelihood Development Program of Hijra (transgender) Community*. Dhaka: Ministry of Social Welfare, People's Republic of Bangladesh.

MissMalini (2015), "This Video of Hijras Singing Jana Gana Mana is Definitely the Most Impactful Independence Day Video This Year." *MissMalini.com*, August 13. https://www.missmalini.com/2015/08/13/this-video-of-hijras-singing-jana-gana-mana-is-definitely-the-most-impactful-independence-day-video-this-year (accessed January 15, 2021).

Mittermaier, Amira (2011), *Dreams that Matter: Egyptian Landscapes of Imagination*. Berkeley: University of California Press.

Morcom, Anna (2014), *Illicit Worlds of Indian Dance: Cultures of Exclusion*. New York: Oxford University Press.

Mount, Liz (2020), "'I Am Not a Hijra': Class, Respectability, and the Emergence of the 'New' Transgender Woman in India." *Gender & Society* 34, no. 4: 620–47.

Nagar, Ila (2020), *Being Janana: Language and Sexuality in Contemporary India*. London: Routledge.

Nanda, Serena ([1990] 1999), *Neither Man, nor Woman: The Hijras of India*. Belmont, CA: Wadsworth Publishing Company.

Naqvi, Nauman, and Hasan Mujtaba (1997), "Two Baluchi *Baggas*, a Sindhi *Zenana* and the Status of *Hijras* in Contemporary Pakistan." In *Islamic Homosexualities: Culture, History and Literature*, edited by Stephen O. Murray and Will Roscoe, 262–6. New York: New York University Press.

Nataraj, Shakthi (2019), "Trans-formations: Projects of Resignification in Tamil Nadu's Transgender Rights Movement." PhD Diss., University of California, Berkeley.

National Assembly of Pakistan (2018), *Transgender Persons (Protection of Rights) Act*. http://www.na.gov.pk/uploads/documents/1526547582_234.pdf (accessed January 10, 2019).

Ndaliko, Chérie Rivers (2016), *Necessary Noise: Music, Film, and Charitable Imperialism in the East of Congo*. London: Oxford University Press.

NDTV (2015), "Transgenders Singing Jana Gana Mana Remind Us What it Means to be Free." *NDTV.com*, August 14. https://www.ndtv.com/offbeat/transgenders-singing-jana-gana-mana-remind-us-what-it-means-to-be-free-1207271 (accessed January 15, 2021).

Neuman, Daniel (1990), *The Life of Music in North India*. Chicago: The University of Chicago Press.

Neuman, Dard (2004), "A House of Music: The Hindustani Musician and the Crafting of Traditions." PhD Diss., Columbia University.

Ochoa, Marcia (2014), *Queen for a Day: Transformistas, Beauty Queens, and the Performance of Femininity in Venezuela*. Durham, NC: Duke University Press.

Oxfam in Pakistan (2018), "For the first time in Pakistan's history ..." *Twitter*, July 23. https://twitter.com/OxfaminPakistan/status/1021340066512334848/photo/1 (accessed July 25, 2018).

Pamment, Claire (2010), "Hijraism: Jostling for a Third Space in Pakistani Politics." *TDR: The Drama Review* 54, no. 2: 29–50.

Pamment, Claire (2012), "A Split Discourse: Body Politics in Pakistan's Popular Punjabi Theatre." *TDR: The Drama Review* 56, no. 1: 114–27.

Pamment, Claire (2015), "Dancing at the Edges of Section 377: *Hijraism* in South Asia." *The Life and Future of British Colonial Sexual Regulation in Asia*. NUS: Singapore, October 8–9, 2015.

Pamment, Claire (2017), *Comic Performance in Pakistan: The* Bhānd. London: Palgrave.

Pamment, Claire (2019a), "Performing Piety in Pakistan's Transgender Rights Movement." *Transgender Studies Quarterly* 6, no. 3: 297–314.

Pamment, Claire (2019b), "The Hijra Clap in Neoliberal Hands: Performing Trans Activism in Pakistan." *TDR: The Drama Review* 63, no. 1: 141–51.

Pamment, Claire with Anaya Rahimi, Malik Ammarr and Umar Jilani (2019c), *Vadhai*. Pamment and Knapsack Studios. https://youtu.be/e7MwJvhtDOw (accessed November 24, 2021).

Pamment, Claire, Iram Sana, Naghma Gogi, Neeli Rana, Jannat Ali, Anaya Rahimi, Lucky Khan, and Sunniya Abbasi (2015), *Teesri Dhun (The Third Tune)*. Social Sciences and Humanities Research of Canada and Olomopolo Media, Alhamra Lahore.

Pamment, Claire, Iram Sana, Naghma Gogi, Neeli Rana, Jannat
    Ali, Anaya Sheikh, Lucky Khan, and Sunniya Abbasi (2021),
    "A Conversation: The *Third Tune (Teesri Dhun)*." In *The
    Routledge Companion to Applied Performance*, edited by Tim
    Prentki and Ananda Breed, 215–27. London: Routledge.
Pamment, Claire (forthcoming a), "On the Other Side of the
    Rainbow? Khwaja Siras and the Tablighi Jama'at." In *Pak*stan
    Desires: Queer Futures Elsewhere*, edited by Omar Kasmani.
    Durham, NC: Duke University Press.
Pamment, Claire (forthcoming b), "Mediatizing 'Fake' Khwaja
    Siras: The Limits of Impersonation." *In Mimetic Desires:
    Impersonation and Guising across South Asia*, edited by Harshita
    Mruthinti Kamath and Pamela Lothspeich. Hawaii: University of
    Hawaii Press.
Pandian, Anand (2019), *A Possible Anthropology: Methods for
    Uneasy Times*. Durham, NC: Duke University Press.
Peletz, Michael G. (2006), "Transgenderism and Gender Pluralism
    in Southeast Asia since Early Modern Times." *Current
    Anthropology* 47, no. 2: 309–40.
Porosh, Sahadat Hossain (2021), "Jongi Shonghotoner target tritiyo
    linger manush." *Samakal*, March 9. https://www.samakal.com/
    bangladesh/article/210355180/জঙ্গি-সংগঠনের-টার্গেটে-তৃতীয়-
    লিঙ্গের-মানুষ (accessed August 20, 2021).
Prakash, Brahma (2019), *Cultural Labour: Conceptualizing the
    "Folk Performance" in India*. New York: Oxford University
    Press.
Prakash, Brahma (2021), "Archives are a SCAM!" *Contemporary
    Theatre Review*. https://www.contemporarytheatrereview.
    org/2021/archives-are-a-scam/
Prasad, Pavithra (2020a), "A Spectral Genealogy of Performance in
    Intercultural Communication Studies." *Journal of Intercultural
    Communication Research* 49, no. 5: 416–24.
Prasad, Pavithra (2020b), "From Lemuria to Wakanda: Speculative
    Cartography from the Deep." Lecture-Performance. Yadunandan
    Center for Indian Studies, February 24, 2020.
Prasad, Pavithra, and Jeff Roy (2017), "Ethnomusicology and
    Performance Studies: Towards Interdisciplinary Futures of Indian
    Classical Music." *MUSICultures* 44, no. 1: 187–209.

Prasad, Pavithra and Jeff Roy, co-chairs (2018), "Un/desirable Encounters at the Intersections of Race, Class and Caste." 3rd Queer Symposium at the Annual Conference on South Asia.

Puar, Jasbir, ed. (2012), "Precarity Talk: A Virtual Roundtable with Lauren Berlant, Judith Butler, Bojana Cvejić, Isabell Lorey, Jasbir Puar, and Ana Vujanović." *TDR: The Drama Review* 56, no. 4: 163–77.

Puri, Jyoti (2010), "Transgendering Development: Reframing Hijras and Development." In *Development, Sexual Rights and Global Governance*, edited by Amy Lind, 39–53. London: Routledge.

Puri, Jyoti (2016), *Sexual States: Governance and the Struggle over the Antisodomy Law in India*. Durham, NC: Duke University Press.

Putcha, Rumya (forthcoming), *The Dancer's Voice: Performance and Womanhood in Transnational India*. Durham, NC: Duke University Press.

Qureshi, Ayaz (2018), *AIDS in Pakistan: Bureaucracy, Public Goods, and NGOs*. Singapore: Palgrave Macmillan.

Qureshi, Regula (2007), *Master Musicians of India*. New York: Routledge.

Racy, Ali Jihad (2004), *Musik Making in the Arab World: The Culture and Artistry of Tarab*. London: Cambridge University Press.

Rashid, Maria (2020), *Dying to Serve: Militarism, Affect, and the Politics of Sacrifice in the Pakistan Army*. Stanford, CA: Stanford University Press.

Redding, Jeffrey, A. (2019), "The Pakistan Transgender Persons (Protection of Rights) Act of 2018 and its Impact on the Law of Gender in Pakistan." *Australian Journal of Asian Law* 20, no. 1: 103–13.

Redding, Jeffrey A. (2021), "Surveillance, Censure and Support: Gender Counting in South Asia." *South Asia: Journal of South Asian Studies* 44, no. 6: 1056–74.

Reddy, Gayatri (2003), "'Men' Who Would Be Kings: Celibacy, Emasculation, and the Re-Production of *Hijras* in Contemporary Indian Politics." *Social Research: An International Quarterly* 70, no. 1: 163–200.

Reddy, Gayatri (2005), *With Respect to Sex: Negotiating Hijra Identity in South India*. Chicago: The University of Chicago Press.

Reddy, Gayatri (2018), "Paradigms of Thirdness: Analyzing the Past, Present, and Potential Futures of Gender and Sexual Meaning in India." *QED: A Journal in GLBTQ Worldmaking* 5, no. 3: 48–60.

Reema and Sana (2014), Vadhai performance. Lahore, February 20.

Reema (2019), Interview with Pamment. Lahore, August 26.

Robinson, Dylan (2020), *Hungry Listening*. Minneapolis, MN: University of Minnesota Press.

Roy, Jeff, director (2011), *Invisible Goddesses*, film.

Roy, Jeff, director (2011–12), *Rites of Passage/Mohammed to Maya*, films.

Roy, Jeff (2012–13), *Music in Liminal Spaces*, digital media and documentary film series. Fulbright-mtvU Fellows. https://mtvufulbright.wordpress.com/author/mtvujroy/

Roy, Jeff (2015a), "Ethnomusicology of the Closet: (Con)Figuring Transgender-*Hijra* Identity through Documentary Filmmaking." PhD Diss., University of California, Los Angeles.

Roy, Jeff (2015b), "The 'Dancing Queens': Negotiating Hijra Pehchān from India's Streets onto the Global Stage." *Ethnomusicology Review* 20: 1–23.

Roy, Jeff, director (2015c), "India's Big Push for Transgender and Hijra Welfare." Co-produced by India HIV/AIDS Alliance. https://www.youtube.com/watch?v=mJB6Sl63lSI (accessed July 15, 2021).

Roy, Jeff, director (2015d), "Dancing Queens: It's All About Family." Documentary film and performance event choreographed by Abheena Aher and the Dancing Queens. Co-produced by Fulbright-Hays and Godrej India Culture Lab.

Roy, Jeff (2016), "Translating *Hijra* into Transgender: Performance and *Pehchān* in India's Trans-*Hijra* Communities." *Transgender Studies Quarterly* 3, no. 3–4: 412–32.

Roy, Jeff (2017), "From Jalsah to Jalsā: Music, Identity, and (Gender) Transitioning at a Hījṛā Rite of Initiation." *Ethnomusicology* 61, no. 3: 389–418.

Roy, Jeff (2018), "Introduction: Queer Forum on Navigating Normativity between Field and Academe in India." *QED: A Journal in GLBTQ Worldmaking* 5, no. 3: 42–7.

Roy, Jeff (2019a), "Con/Figuring Transgender-Hijra Music and Dance through Queer Ethnomusicological Filmmaking." In *Queering the Field: Sounding Out Ethnomusicology*, edited by Gregory Barz and William Cheng, 163–84. London: Oxford University Press.

Roy, Jeff (2019b), "Remapping the Voice through Transgender-Hījṛā Performance." In *Remapping Sound Studies*, edited by Gavin

Steingo and Jim Sykes, 173–82. Durham, NC: Duke University Press.

Roy, Jeff (forthcoming), "Music and the Trans-*thirunangai* Everyday at Koovagam, Tamil Nadu." In *Music and Dance as Everyday South Asia*, edited by Sarah Morelli and Zoe Sherinian. New York: Oxford University Press.

Roy, Jeff, Pavithra Prasad, Rumya Putcha, and Omar Kasmani (forthcoming), "Introduction: Un/Desirable Journeys ←→ Queer Elsewheres: South Asian Imaginaries across Intersectional Terrain." Guest-Edited Themed Issue of *Feminist Review* 133.

Saadat, Syed Yusuf (2018), "Rehabilitating the Beggars." *The Financial Express*, January 19. https://thefinancialexpress.com.bd/views/views/rehabilitating-the-beggars-1516373489 (accessed November 20, 2020).

Sachdeva, Shweta (2008), "In Search of the Tawa'if in History: Courtesans, Nautch Girls and Celebrity Entertainers in India (1720s–1920s)." PhD Diss., SOAS, University of London, London.

Said, Edward (1978), *Orientalism*. New York: Pantheon Books.

Sapte, B. (1865), IOR/P/483/61, February 17, 1866, No. 21. From Officiating Commissioner, Agra Division, to Secretary to Government, North-Western Provinces, Allahabad (No. 1045). Dated Agra, September 16, 1865.

Saria, Vaibhav (2019), "Begging for Change: Hijras, Law and Nationalism." *Contributions to Indian Sociology* 53, no. 1: 133–57.

Saria, Vaibhav (2021), *Hijras, Lovers, Brothers: Surviving Sex and Poverty in Rural India*. New York: Fordham University Press.

Savigliano, Marta Elina (2009), "Worlding Dance and Dancing Out There in the World." In *Worlding Dance: Studies in International Performance*, edited by Susan Leigh Foster, 163–90. London: Palgrave Macmillan.

Schechner, Turner (1985), *Between Theater and Anthropology*. Philadelphia: University of Pennsylvania Press.

Schendel, Willem van (2007), *A History of Bangladesh*. Cambridge: Cambridge University Press.

Seizer, Susan (2005), *Stigmas of the Tamil Stage: An Ethnography of Special Drama Artists in South India*. Durham, NC: Duke University Press.

Senelick, Laurence (2000), *The Changing Room: Sex, Drag and Theatre*. London; New York: Routledge.

Sengupta, Durga M. (2017), "I Am Not a Hijra: A Damaging, Offensive Transgender India Photo Campaign." *CatchNews*, February 10. https://www.catchnews.com/gender-and-sex/i-am-not-a-hijra-a-damaging-offensive-transgender-india-photo-campaign-1471618717.html (accessed January 15, 2021).

Shroff, Sara (2020), "Operationalizing the 'New' Pakistani Transgender Citizen: Legal Gendered Grammars and Trans Frames of Feeling." In *Gender, Sexuality, Decolonization: South Asia in the World Perspective*, edited by Ahonaa Roy, 260–82. Abingdon, Oxon; New York: Routledge.

Slaby, Jan, Rainer Mühlhoff, and Philipp Wüschner (2019), "Affective Arrangements." *Emotion Review* 11, no. 1: 3–12.

Spivak, Gayatri Chakravorty (1993), *Outside in the Teaching Machine*. New York: Routledge.

Soneji, Davesh (2011), *Unfinished Gestures: Devadasis, Memory, and Modernity in South India*. Chicago: The University of Chicago Press.

Soneji, Davesh (forthcoming), *Sundry Ragas: Genealogies of Musical Pluralism in Modern South India*.

Srinivasan, Amrit (1985), "Reform and Revival: The Devadasi and Her Dance." *Economic and Political Weekly* 20, no. 44: 1869–76.

Srinivasan, Priya (2012), *Sweating Saris: Indian Dance as Transnational Labor*. Philadelphia, PA: Temple University Press.

Stokes, Whitley (1870), "Whitley Stokes, Sec. to the Govt. of India." 419–427, October 3, 1870. In BL/IOR/V/9/11-12.

Supreme Court of Pakistan (2009), Constitutional Petition No. 43 of 2009, February 6. On file with Claire Pamment.

Sutherland, John (2018), *Literary Landscape: Charting the Worlds of Classic Literature*. New York: Black Dog and Leventhal Publishers.

Talwar, Tanvi, director (2011), *Between the Two*, film.

Taylor, Diana (2003), *The Archive and the Repertoire: Performing Cultural Memory in the Americas*. Durham, NC: Duke University Press.

Taylor, Diana (2020), *¡Presente!: The Politics of Presence*. Durham, NC: Duke University Press,

TNM (2018), "LGBTQIA+ community condemns trans activist Laxmi Narayan Tripathi's Ram temple comment." *The News Minute*, November 24. https://www.thenewsminute.com/article/

lgbtqia-community-condemns-trans-activist-laxmi-narayan-tripathis-ram-temple-comment-92152 (accessed December 23, 2020).

Tom, Liza, and Shilpa Menon (2021), "Living with the Norm: The Nirvanam Ritual in South Indian Transfeminine Narratives of Self and Transition." *GLQ: A Journal of Lesbian and Gay Studies* 27, no. 1: 39–59.

Towle, Evan B., and Lynn Marie Morgan (2002), "Romancing the Transgender Native: Rethinking the Use of the 'Third Gender' Concept." *GLQ: A Journal of Lesbian and Gay Studies* 8, no. 4: 469–97.

Trans News (2021a), "Sharia ..." *Trans News*, May 5. https://www.facebook.com/Transnewspk/videos/308610964225431 (accessed May 5, 2021).

Trans News (2021b), "Arzoo ..." *Trans News*, May 11. https://www.facebook.com/Transnewspk/videos/507177333792407 (accessed May 11, 2021).

Trans News (2021c), "Azad Dera ...." *Trans News*, June 28. https://www.facebook.com/Transnewspk/videos/848786686039355 (accessed June 28, 2021).

Tripathi, Dhananjay, and Sanjay Chaturvedi (2020), "South Asia: Boundaries, Borders and Beyond." *Journal of Borderlands Studies* 35, no. 2: 173–81.

Tuck, Eve, and K. W. Yang (2012), "Decolonization is Not a Metaphor." *Decolonization: Indigeneity, Education & Society* 1, no. 1: 1–40.

Tyrwhitt (1878), P/1138: Tyrwhitt to Sec, NWP&O, May 28, 1878. No 655A, From Col. E. Tyrwhitt, Insptr Gen. Police NWp and O to Sec Gov NWP and Oudh. Annual Report of 1877 on Working of Criminal Tribes.

Ung Loh, J. (2014), "Narrating Identity: The Employment of Mythological and Literary Narratives in Identity Formation among the *Hijras* of India." *Religion & Gender* 4, no. 1: 21–39.

Upadhyay, Nishant (2020), "Hindu Nation and its Queers: Caste, Islamophobia, and De/coloniality in India." *International Journal of Postcolonial Studies* 22, no. 4: 464–80.

Vasudevan, Aniruddhan (2020), "Between the Goddess and the World: Religion and Ethics among Thirunangai Transwomen in Chennai, India." PhD Diss., University of Texas at Austin.

Vikram, Anuradha (2019), "Degrees of Privilege: A Conversation on Race, Caste, and Access in the Diaspora with Jaishri Abichandani, Rina Banerjee, Neha Choksi, and Sandeep Mukherjee." *Asian Diasporic Visual Cultures and the Americas* 5, no. 3: 357–68.

Visweswaran, Kamala (1994), *Fictions of Feminist Ethnography*. Minneapolis, MN: University of Minnesota Press.

Voegelin, Salomé (2018), *The Political Possibility of Sound: Fragments of Listening*. New York: Bloomsbury.

Weidman, Amanda (2006), *Singing the Classical, Voicing the Modern: The Postcolonial Politics of Music in South India*. Durham, NC: Duke University Press.

Wimmer, Andreas, and Nina Glick Schiller (2003), "Methodological Nationalism, the Social Sciences, and the Study of Migration: An Essay in Historical Epistemology." *The International Migration Review* 37, no. 3: 576–610.

Zimman, Lal, and Kira Hall (2010), "Language, Embodiment and the 'Third Sex.'" In *Language and Identities*, edited by Carmen Llamas and Dominic Watt, 166–78. Edinburgh: Edinburgh University Press.

INDEX